GARDEN
CRAFTS

BEAUTIFUL CREATIONS
FROM NATURE'S BOUNTY

GARDEN CRAFTS

BEAUTIFUL CREATIONS FROM NATURE'S BOUNTY

CREATIVE
HOME
ARTS
MINNETONKA —CLUB— MINNESOTA

CREDITS

Garden Crafts
Beautiful Creations from Nature's Bounty

Tom Carpenter
Creative Director

Michele Stockham
Senior Book Development Coordinator

Heather Koshiol
Managing Editor

Zachary Marell
Book Design & Production

Contributing Writers
Zoe Graul
Cheryl Nelson
Cheryl Natt
Nancy Maurer
Jana Freiband
Ellen Spector Platt

Photography
Phil Aarrestad Photography

Additional Photography
Alan and Linda Detrick Photography

The following material in this book is used under license from International Masters Publishers, Inc: Projects starting on pages 26, 36, 40, 46, 50, 54, 130, 134, 144.

1 2 3 4 5 6 / 07 06 05 04 03
ISBN 1-58159-204-3

Creative Home Arts Club
12301 Whitewater Drive
Minnetonka, MN 55343
www.creativehomeartsclub.com

CONTENTS

INTRODUCTION

A Natural Combination: Craft Fun and Garden Beauty

By themselves, the arts of crafting and gardening are enjoyable enough. But combine the two pastimes and you get some of the most exciting crafting, decorating, cooking and gift-giving ideas you will ever see.

Garden Crafts makes that tie for you, bringing together dozens of attractive projects you can create, each one utilizing products of the garden or nature, or celebrating the glory of the garden's beauty.

Because time is limited these days but you still want to achieve success on every craft, we've presented each idea in a clear, concise and easy-to-follow format. It starts with a vibrant color photo of the finished creation, offers plenty of background facts (including detailed tools and materials lists) to get you going, continues with step-by-step how-to-do-it instructions that are photographed in full color, and ends with plenty of tips, hints, notes and insights that help you complete every item without a hitch.

Start indoors, and see how you can bring the garden's beauty into your home. Take some time to create crafts that decorate and beautify your outdoor living space too.

Discover garden crafts—some you decorate with, some you eventually eat!—for *and* from the kitchen. Put some lovely fragrances into your life. And fashion great gift-giving items that will be uniquely from you.

Anyone who loves a little natural beauty will love this book. These *Garden Crafts* are easy, fun and affordable to make … and they truly are *Beautiful Creations from Nature's Bounty*. You're going to enjoy making the projects in this book and love the end results … naturally!

INDOOR

*B*ring the beauty of the garden indoors! This chapter shows you how ... with flowers you grow or buy, and items from nature too. But you'll also discover how to create crafts with a garden theme, and then use them to help decorate in fresh and inviting ways. From dried fresh flowers to a variety of gorgeous wreaths, and from elegant floral frames to garden boxes, decorator pillows and much more, these ideas and instructions will keep your hands busy creating great garden crafts you will enjoy in every room of your home.

WEATHERED WOOD MINIATURE BENCH FOR FLOWERPOTS

Weathered wood adds charm to a project and any irregularities in the wood only enhance the final product.

BEFORE YOU BEGIN

Working with weathered wood may mean that every edge and corner may not line up perfectly since warping is common in weathered wood. When making decisions on the placement of the wood pieces, use warping or other irregularities to an advantage. The piece of board used in this project is 8 inches by 1 inch. The project could also be made of cedar or pine board. The size of the board would be different so slight adjustments would need to be made on measurements and amount of wood needed.

The only cost for this project is the wood and nails and is minimal. It takes a couple of hours to do, depending on your sawing and nailing ability. The final dimensions of the bench are 11 inches long, by 9 inches high, by about $5\frac{3}{4}$ inches deep.

This miniature bench, made of weathered wood, provides a unique background for two small potted plants. The holes will accommodate a standard 3-inch clay pot. The contrast in both color and texture will work nicely with the natural greenery or the color of the blooms. One pot can be used and a stuffed animal or antique doll can be put in the other space to add more interest.

TOOLS NEEDED
- ❑ DRILL
- ❑ SMALL DRILL BIT FOR STARTING NAIL HOLES
- ❑ $\frac{3}{8}$-INCH DRILL BIT FOR USE WITH JIG SAW TO CUT CIRCLES
- ❑ HAMMER
- ❑ JIG SAW OR DRILL PRESS WITH 3-INCH HOLE SAW
- ❑ TABLE OR RADIAL-ARM SAW

MATERIALS NEEDED
- ❑ WEATHERED BOARD MEASURING 8 INCHES BY 1 INCH BY 32 INCHES
- ❑ $1\frac{1}{2}$-INCH FINISHING NAILS—ABOUT 20

HOW TO MAKE A WEATHERED WOOD MINIATURE BENCH FOR FLOWERPOTS

2 Top of bench measures 3¼ inches from work surface. Mark nail placement on side pieces 2¾ inches from bottom and 1 inch from side edges. Drill pilot holes for nails. Place side piece next to end of bench, with top of bench measuring 3¼ inches from bottom edge of side piece. Remember to have the weathered edge as top and front edge of side, and front edge of bench. Nail in place. Repeat process for other side.

1 Mark and cut the following pieces, according to layout, to be able to use weathered edges as much as possible. For seat of bench—9 inches by 4¾ inches; for sides—two pieces each 6 inches by 3¾ inches; for front rail—11½ inches by 1 inch; for back rail—9 inches by 1 inch; for back pickets—four pieces at 9 inches by 2¼ inches, cut to a 90-degree-angle point on one end of each. Mark the circles 1 inch in from sides, leaving about 1 inch between circles and about ¾ inch from both front and back edge. Cut the 2 circles on the bench with a 3-inch hole saw on a drill press or with a jig saw. Using the drill press is the easiest and will make a perfect circle, however the circles do not need to be perfect as the clay pots will cover them. When using the jig saw, make 4 equidistant drill holes around the edge of the circle and about ⅜ inch in diameter. Then cut with jig saw around marked line.

3 Place front rail across front of bench at lower edge. The outside edge of the rail extends over sides about ¼ inch. Drill pilot hole in rail about ¾ inch in from ends. Nail in place.

4 Place back rail on back side of bench, between the sides and lining up flush with side and bottom edges. Drill pilot hole about ½ inch from each edge of the side piece. Nail in place.

5 Place the first outside picket flush along side piece and bottom rail. Be sure to use a weathered edge of picket to the outside of bench. Drill pilot holes at bottom outside corner, 5½ inches from bottom and 2¾ inches near the inside edge of picket. Each hole should be about ½ inch from edge of picket. Nail in place.

6 Place the two remaining pickets in place. There should be about ½ inch between each one. Drill pilot holes centered in pickets and ½ inch and 2¾ inches from bottom edge, to go into the back rail and bench back. Nail in place.

HANDY HINTS

Place a mini watering can on the bench or arm rest for a fun look.

Attach an artificial bird, butterfly or bug on a picket or arm rest, for an extra embellishment.

OOPS!

Sometimes the process of **nailing** one piece loosens other pieces. Keep checking for any shifting, before doing each piece, since they need to be spaced evenly. Repeat for outside picket, making sure a weathered edge is to the outside.

TRUE BLUE CYANOTYPE

*Use favorite plants or flowers from your garden
to create a lasting memory with Cyanotype.*

BEFORE YOU BEGIN

A vibrant Prussian blue, known since the 1800s as Cyanotype, is
created by the action of sunlight on iron-salt chemicals, producing the
truest of blue backgrounds with a white negative image. A history of
Victorian gardens and plants exists today from Cyanotype images
made by past Botanical Societies.

The process involves designing objects on top of a light-sensitized
Cyanotype material. When placed in the sun, the background
becomes darker, leaving the areas covered by objects light. After
exposure, placed in water and completely rinsed, the background
turns a vivid blue and the design becomes a brilliant white.

A lasting botanical memory of your garden can easily be created on
a variety of papers and fabrics. Plant leaves, flowers and branches
can all be used in creating a design. A flat silhouette, or an artistic
floral blur can be made by moving objects during the exposure time.
The sun is the source, as in the garden, of activating the process and
watching it become true blue.

MATERIALS NEEDED
❏ SENSITIZED CYANOTYPE
   MATERIALS (AVAILABLE AT
   SOME ART STORES, OR
   INTERNET SOURCE
   WWW.FREESTYLEPHOTO.BIZ)
❏ FORM CORE BOARD TO
   SIZE OF CYANOTYPE
   MATERIAL
❏ EMPTY BOX
❏ GLASS SHEET TO SIZE
❏ VARIETY OF OBJECTS:
   PLANT LEAVES, FLOWERS,
   BRANCHES,
❏ GARDEN EDGING

TOOLS NEEDED
❏ STRAIGHT PINS
❏ TRAY FOR WATER

HOW TO MAKE TRUE BLUE CYANOTYPE

1 In subdued indoor light, remove Cyanotype material from protective dark bag. Place sheet on form core inside empty box. Arrange objects on surface. Cover with glass if you want a direct silhouette image. For objects that will not fit under glass or objects you would like to move during the exposure time, use pins to attach in place.

2 Cover box lightly with a sheet of newspaper and place in direct sunlight. Exposure time will vary depending on time of day, time of year, weather and location. At the end of your exposure time cover your design with newspaper and return to subdued light.

TAKE NOTE

You can create a more abstract image by moving the objects every 5 minutes during the exposure time.

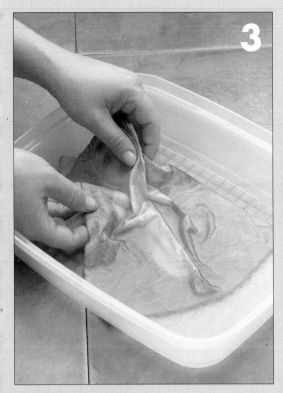

3

3 Remove objects on surface and rinse Cyanotype material in water tray until water runs clear. Hang or place to dry. The final color will not be seen until after rinsing and drying.

4 What to do with your final designs? Frame them, sew them on a pillow or curtain, or make a quilt. Gather them together and make your own botanical diary.

4

GILDED LEAVES

TOOL NEEDED
❏ PAINTBRUSH

Gilding leaves is a simple technique that produces beautiful golden leaves to decorate gift packages, candle holders, stationery or to be used to embellish a label on a jar of canned preserves, vinegar or salsa.

MATERIALS NEEDED
❏ STURDY LEAVES SUCH AS DRIED BAY LEAF OR LEMON LEAVES
❏ VARIEGATED GOLD LEAF
❏ SPRAY ADHESIVE
❏ STRAIGHT PINS

BEFORE YOU BEGIN

Who doesn't love the elegance of gold? Gilding leaves is a simple and fairly inexpensive way to use nature's bounty to create simple, yet beautiful, decorations. Gilding requires very few tools and a little variegated gold leaf that will go a long way. To dress up candle holders for an elegant and festive dinner party wrap them in gilded grape leaves and tie with a silk ribbon to dress up the dinner table, or use them to decorate place cards with dinner guests' names on them. There are numerous ways to use this wonderfully simple craft. Don't limit your gilding to leaves alone; experiment with miniature squash or pumpkins also.

HANDY HINTS

Protect your work surface by covering it with newspaper or freezer paper before working with the spray adhesive, or work outside to avoid making a mess.

Variegated gold leaf comes in different colors such as copper or gold and can be purchased at most fine art supply stores.

2 Lay out one sheet of the variegated gold leaf onto the work surface. Press the sprayed side of the leaf onto the variegated gold leaf sheet. Gently but firmly rub the back side of the leaf. Carefully and gently tear the gilded leaf away from the sheet.

3 Using a paintbrush, brush the leaf to remove any excess flakes. Repeat with opposite side of leaf and continue with other leaves.

1 Pin the edges of the leaves to a large piece of cardboard using the straight pins to hold them securely in place. Spray a thin coat of the adhesive spray on one side of the leaf.

TAKE NOTE

Use the gold leaves to embellish potpourri, flower arrangements or as decorative accents for stationery, tables or gift packages.

Be sure to use a clean, dry paintbrush to brush the leaves. A damp brush will remove the variegated gold leaf from the leaves.

Look for different sizes and shapes of leaves for more interest. Grape leaves, lemon leaves, bay leaves or even small pressed flowers will work well.

Variegated gold leaf is not edible and should be kept away from food to be eaten.

FOUR CREATIONS FROM STICKS AND STONES

Mother Nature provides the materials. You provide the creative thought to bring nature home.

BEFORE YOU BEGIN

Take a walk in the woods, head to the beach, look out your back door in your garden; everything you need for this project is close at hand. Collect fallen branches or stones along a path and see what new uses you can find for them. These four projects—a soap dish (pictured at left), curtain rod, drawer pull and tick-tack-toe game—really help you bring nature home. And what better way to commemorate a vacation or getaway (or even honor a wild place you love), than with a creation from materials you bring home?

TOOLS NEEDED
❏ SEE THE DETAILED LIST WITH EACH OF THE FOUR PROJECTS.

MATERIALS NEEDED
❏ SEE THE DETAILED LIST WITH EACH OF THE FOUR PROJECTS.

HOW TO MAKE FOUR STICKS AND STONES CREATIONS

Collected Sticks Soap Dish

Curtain Rod

1 Shape of the stick creates the interest in this project. Choose a stick, measure to length of window frame, adding several inches on the ends for visual effect. Peel or chisel away bark, then sand to make a smooth even surface. Fabric curtain can be draped or hung from the finished stick. Use two hooks on each end of top window frame to hang. Extended ends of stick can be left natural or decorated with leaves or vines.

TOOLS NEEDED
❑ WOOD CHISEL
❑ SANDPAPER

MATERIALS NEEDED
❑ BRANCH, CURVED OR STRAIGHT FORM
❑ SCREW HOOK OR ROBE HOOK TO ATTACH TO WINDOW FRAME

Collected Sticks Soap Dish

1 Collected sticks can be measured for length and width for the size of dish you choose. Saw off even lengths. Smooth surface by peeling or chiseling sticks' bark, than sand. Group sticks so they fit close together. Measure 1 inch down from each end; use drill to make holes on the sides going through all sticks. Measure width of all sticks together; cut two sticks to use as joiners. Match sticks' diameter to the size of the drilled holes. Insert joiner sticks through all holes, one to each end. Spray with polyurethane coating to finish.

TOOLS NEEDED
❑ WOOD CHISEL
❑ SANDPAPER
❑ SAW
❑ DRILL

MATERIALS NEEDED
❑ STICKS
❑ POLYURETHANE SATIN SPRAY COATING

Curtain Rod

Stone Pulls

Tick, Tack Toe, Sticks and Stones

1 Cut four equal lengths of sticks. Cross two on two to form nine squares. Tie center four sticks together, wrapping twine around two sides to keep all sticks in place. Three stones in a row wins!

MATERIALS NEEDED
- ❑ STICKS
- ❑ TWO DIFFERENT COLORS OF SMALL STONES, FIVE OF EACH COLOR
- ❑ GARDEN TWINE

Stone Pulls

1 Choose smooth flat stones, measure a small stick to size of width of the stone. Cut a piece of twine 5x length of stone. Tightly tie the twine to stone; tie once, then insert stick and tie again to keep tight contact. Take the two ends of the twine and pull them through a hole made in drawer or cabinet. Pull twine to inside, tie once, then again tie a small stick to anchor the pull.

MATERIALS NEEDED
- ❑ SMOOTH FLAT STONES
- ❑ SMALL STICK PIECES
- ❑ GARDEN TWINE

Tick, Tack Toe, Sticks and Stones

PERSONALIZED GARDEN JOURNAL

TOOLS NEEDED
- ❏ GLUE GUN
- ❏ LARGE-EYED TAPESTRY NEEDLE
- ❏ AWL
- ❏ HAMMER
- ❏ DRILL
- ❏ DRILL BIT THAT ACCOMMODATES TAPESTRY NEEDLE

It is fun to keep a garden journal or one that even includes weather, bird and animal related notes. This can also be a great gift item, as you can personalize it.

BEFORE YOU BEGIN

To keep with the contents of the journal, it can be embellished with natural elements, such as birch bark, twigs, rocks or cedar sprigs. Try to keep the elements fairly flat and enduring. The journal that is embellished can be a simple notebook or a more elaborate one; however, most of the cover will be embellished. The cardboard back of the notebook can be used because it is heavy enough and neutral in color. A bookmark can be put on the back cover and be embellished.

This project will cost the amount of the notebook, which can vary, and the cost of letters, which can be press-on ones or, if calligraphy is a skill you have, do the lettering yourself. The minimum cost would be about $3.00 for the simplest notebook, plus letters, which may cost $4.00 to $5.00. The project will take less than an hour, including drying time. Do not harvest birch bark or other natural elements out of state or national parks.

MATERIALS NEEDED
- ❏ BIRCH BARK
- ❏ BIRCH OR WILLOW TWIG —ABOUT $3/8$ INCH IN DIAMETER
- ❏ RAFFIA
- ❏ ROCK AND OTHER NATURAL ELEMENTS SUCH AS CEDAR SPRIGS OR SMALL PINECONES
- ❏ COPPER WIRE—ABOUT 18 GAUGE, AND ABOUT 6 INCHES IN LENGTH

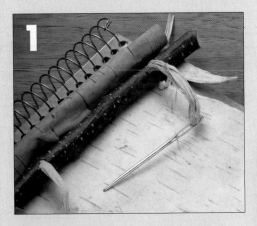

2 Cut a flat piece of birch bark, large enough to accommodate the lettering and fit nicely on the journal. Use the back side of the bark; it is usually smoother and more consistent in color. Line up letters, as desired, and adhere them, according to manufacturer's instructions. Place on journal and secure by either gluing or making holes and stitching, as in step one.

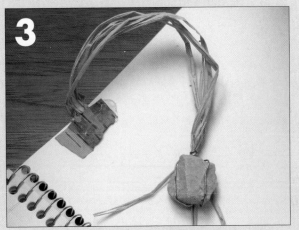

1 Decide on placement of all elements for cover of journal. Take advantage of the natural elements' lines; parts may even extend over cover. Instead of cutting the birch bark, tear it, in order to keep with the natural look. Use glue gun to glue birch bark in place. Put something heavy on cover as it dries. Cut twig to desired size and drill two holes in it. Place twig where desired, open cover and place it over a wood block. Put awl through hole in twig and pound through cover. Repeat for other hole. Thread one strand of raffia through tapestry needle and starting from outside go though one hole and back to outside through other hole. Tie a bow and trim raffia ends to desired length. Add any other embellishments desired.

3 To make the bookmark, fold a piece of raffia into four equal portions that are long enough to cross journal and extend on both ends by a few inches. Wrap wire around a nicely shaped flat rock and then around one end of the raffia. Glue the other end of raffia to the inside back cover of journal, using the glue gun. Cut a small piece of bark and glue it over the end of raffia.

HANDY HINTS

To remove any glue tendrils from the journal, use a hair dryer to dissolve them.

DRYING FRESH FLOWERS

Silica gel preserves the vivid colors and delicate forms of fresh flowers.

BEFORE YOU BEGIN

Silica gel is a powdery, sand-like substance that dries flowers in a few days. The colors dry brilliant and clear and the shapes are preserved in their original state.

Silica gel works by absorbing moisture from the flowers, much like a sponge would. As it does, the blue dots in the mixture turn pink. When this happens, it means that the silica gel has absorbed its maximum moisture content and needs to be dried.

To reactivate the silica gel, spread it out in a thin layer on a flat baking dish. Dry in a warm oven (250 to 300°F) for about 30 minutes or until the crystals turn blue again.

The diagram below outlines what kinds of flowers were used where, in the arrangement at left.

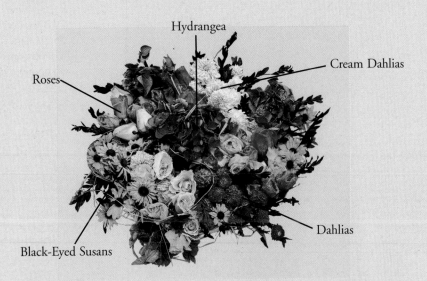

Hydrangea

Cream Dahlias

Roses

Dahlias

Black-Eyed Susans

HOW TO DRY FRESH FLOWERS

1 Select flowers to be dried just before they reach full bloom. Most flowers dried in full bloom tend to fall apart when dry. Use sharp scissors to cut the flower stems to within 1 inch of the flower heads.

2 Pour some silica gel crystals into a plastic container to fill it about halfway. Place flowers face up in the silica gel. With a spoon, gently sprinkle some of the gel around and between flower petals.

3 Cover the flowers completely with the silica gel crystals. Seal the container with an airtight lid. Let the flowers dry for two to seven days, checking daily to make sure you do not overdry them.

OOPS!

If a flower petal falls off in the silica gel mixture, just apply a dab of white glue and carefully glue petal back onto the flower.

TAKE NOTE

Use empty coffee cans with plastic lids when drying just a few blossoms, or try airtight plastic dress or shoe boxes for preserving a quantity of flowers.

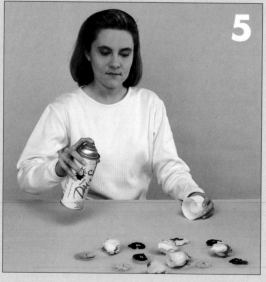

4 When the flowers have dried, remove them by tipping the container and pouring out some of the gel. When the flowers are visible, lift them out one by one from the gel with a slotted spoon.

5 Carefully remove any remaining silica gel crystals from the flower petals with a soft-bristle paintbrush. Then spray the flowers with an aerosol floral sealer, available in florist's shops and craft stores. Preserving them with floral sealer will help to keep the colors looking fresh and bright.

CHOOSING A DRYING METHOD

DRYING OPTIONS	Dahlia	Euphorbia	Larkspur	Lily	Peony	Pansy	Rose	Statice	Stock	Strawflower	Zinnia
SILICA				❀		❀					❀
HANGING		❀	❀					❀		❀	
BOTH	❀				❀		❀		❀		

Bright Ideas: Air-Drying Your Flowers

Air-dry your fresh flowers for a more natural look. The colors soften and the flowers take on a somewhat textured appearance.

Cut and Dried

Gather together some long-stemmed blossoms and hang them up to dry.

• Choose flowers that are best dried hanging upside down as noted in *Before You Begin*.

• Multi-blossom flowers such as delphinium, larkspur, heather and lavender can be dried successfully in bunches.

• Flowers with one large bloom, such as peonies or dahlias, should be hung individually.

• Hang flowers or foliage in a dry, cool, dimly lit place, like a shaded attic eave or a spare closet.

1 Select the flowers to be dried just before they reach full bloom. Remove all of the lower leaves and trim off any damaged areas with scissors.

2 Loosely bundle a bunch of flowers together (about nine to ten stems at the most), staggering the flower heads so that air can evenly circulate around the flowers.

3 Secure the flower bundle near the ends of the stems with raffia or a rubber band. Hang them upside down on a nail to dry for a week or two.

EVERLASTING WREATH KIT

This everlasting wreath kit affords you endless possibilities throughout the seasons.

BEFORE YOU BEGIN

Just as you have a favorite vase or two stashed in a closet, this wreath kit will become an everlasting treasure. When this week's flowers are long gone, the moss-covered wreath, baskets, jars and doilies can be stashed together, ready to retrieve the next time you want a fresh flower or herb display hanging on a wall or door.

If you're looking for a great gift for any flower arranger, assemble the wreath and tie on a little note of instructions. Your friend will think of you each time she or he uses this everlasting wreath kit. It's a great way to bring the garden's glory indoors!

TOOLS NEEDED
- ❏ HOT GLUE GUN AND GLUE STICKS
- ❏ FLORIST'S SPOOL WIRE OR ANY THIN WIRE
- ❏ WIRE CUTTERS
- ❏ FLORAL SHEARS

MATERIALS NEEDED
- ❏ 16-18 INCH STURDY VINE WREATH BASE
- ❏ FIVE HANDFULS GREEN SHEET MOSS OR FIVE MOSS CLUMPS
- ❏ FIVE SMALL BUNCHES FRESH FLOWERS OR HERBS IN SEASON
- ❏ FIVE SMALL BASKETS
- ❏ FIVE BABY FOOD OR SMALL JELLY JARS
- ❏ FIVE DOILIES SIX TO EIGHT INCHES IN DIAMETER OR STARCHED LINEN HANDKERCHIEFS
- ❏ FLORAL FOOD/PRESERVATIVE AND WATER

HOW TO MAKE AN EVERLASTING WREATH KIT

1 Purchase a strong vine wreath base. Hang the wreath on a nail. With the spool wire tie the baskets onto the wreath spacing them evenly. This is easy to do either through little handles on the sides of the basket or poking the wire directly through the weave.

3 Place a doily in each basket making sure that some of the decorative edge drapes over the side of each basket. The back doesn't really matter. Place a small jar in each basket on top of the doily. Add water ¾ of the way to the top with a spouted pitcher or long-necked watering can.

2 With the hot glue gun glue the moss onto the face of the wreath between the baskets. The moss can be added before the baskets if you find that easier.

TAKE NOTE

To make a new wreath use any vine available, like bittersweet, honeysuckle or even better, wisteria. As your wisteria grows it will always need pruning, so use some of those heavy twisted pieces to wrap into a wreath. Do this during the growing season when the vines are pliable. Or if it's a winter project, soak vines overnight in a tub of hot water and in the morning you'll be ready to go to work.

4 Add one type of flower or herb to each basket. Cut the stems short with the floral shears to fit. In the May floral wreath you could use tulips, a few stems of azalea, lilacs, pink dogwood or whatever you have. For the herb wreath, again use whatever is available in any given week. The harvest of May herbs from the garden might include chive flowers, catmint, Scotch broom, wild mustard and sage leaves.

Care of Fresh Flowers

Flowers that are properly cared for last longer. Here's how to get long-lasting beauty. Start with impeccably clean jars each time you use the wreath kit. Condition the flowers in a bucket of lukewarm water to which flower food has been added according to package directions. To condition, recut the stems of the flowers with the floral shears before placing them in the bucket. Strip bottom leaves of the flowers so they don't sit in the water. Then allow to sit in the water about four hours.

• Add water daily to the jars.
• Floral food is available from florists or floral craft stores.
Placement Tips: The flowers will last longer where they can keep their cool. Hang the wreath away from direct sunlight. Also avoid hanging on a door which gets slammed over and over again during the day to avoid water spills. Some front doors rarely get used so this might be a perfect place. Or try an interior door or wall.
Design Tips: Keeping all the flowers in one color range adds some dramatic impact. In the spring floral wreath the selections can be pale pink, hot pink and lilac. In the herb wreath the choices are not by color but by theme: all the selections have a culinary or medicinal use.
• An even easier plan is to use a single type of flower that you have in abundance. Imagine the effect of one huge peony in each jar, or one head of hydrangea, or going smaller, five handfuls of violets. For a wedding or special occasion greet guests with three to five white roses in each jar. For Christmas, sprigs of glossy holly with its crimson berries will keep for several weeks in water. Each choice will offer its own pleasures.

VINE-EMBELLISHED CANDLESTICKS

Revitalize old wooden candlesticks with vine and raffia.

TOOLS NEEDED

❏ WIRE CUTTER
❏ GLUE GUN
❏ TACKS, IF NEEDED

MATERIALS NEEDED

❏ WOODEN CANDLESTICKS, 7 TO 12 INCHES HIGH
❏ VINE—ABOUT 8 TO 9 FEET PER CANDLESTICK DEPENDING ON HEIGHT AND DIAMETER OF CANDLESTICK
❏ RAFFIA
❏ BERRIES OR SMALL EVERGREEN SPRIGS, IF DESIRED
❏ WIRE—ABOUT 18 GAUGE

BEFORE YOU BEGIN

Antique yarn bobbins from woolen mills can also be used for this project by adding a base for the candle on top of the bobbin. Use green vine freshly harvested or purchased artificial vine. Final embellishments can be a raffia bow or a ribbon bow. Berries or small evergreen sprigs may be added to either bow, if desired. Or make these appropriate for the holidays with a red bow or small poinsettia blossom. Be cautious that berries are not toxic to pets or children or use artificial ones. The cost of this project is minimal, only the amount for desired embellishments. If old candlesticks are not available, they can be purchased new or at a resale shop for a minimal expense. This project will take less than an hour.

1 Double-wrap wire around each stem base of three 30- to 36-inch lengths, equally spaced to fit around base of candlestick. If the base is larger in diameter use four lengths of stems. Wrap wire with stems around base and secure by twisting wire. If the candlestick is straight with nothing to hold the wire at base, use tacks to hold wire to bottom of candlestick. These will be covered by raffia later.

2 Begin to wrap and entwine vine up the candlestick to top area. It may be easier to do this by holding the candlestick upside down. At the top, if the candlestick is straight, tack or use glue gun to hold vines in place. If desired, place a piece of raffia with each vine and wrap them together. Continue to wrap densely around top of candlestick. Leave a few tendrils of vine loose for effect. Secure with tacks or glue gun.

3 Wrap raffia or ribbon around top of candlestick to cover glue or tacks and form a bow. Locate the bow to take advantage of vine tendrils as well as to cover glue or tacks. Glue berries or small evergreen sprigs to bow if desired. Also wrap raffia or matching ribbon around bottom area of candle to cover wire. Embellish more if desired.

TAKE NOTE

Metal candlesticks can be used, however wire will be needed to hold grapevine in place. Twist it decoratively to add to the design.

HANDY HINTS

Spray the grapevine lightly with metallic or white paint for a holiday or festive look.

To remove any glue tendrils, use a hair dryer to dissolve them.

DRIED FLOWER TABLETOP TOPIARY

Top a topiary form with dried flowers for an everlasting accent.

BEFORE YOU BEGIN

Whether country or contemporary, subtle or bold, you can make topiaries to complement the color and style of any room in your house.

To make the base, cut the plastic foam block with a knife to fit the shape of the container and then glue the foam in place. Trim the branch to about 10 inches to 12 inches in length. Cut both ends of branch at an angle. Glue one end and push it into center of plastic foam base. The top holds the plastic foam ball.

TOOLS NEEDED

❑ GLUE GUN AND GLUE STICKS
❑ FLORIST'S WIRE
❑ KNIFE AND SCISSORS

MATERIALS NEEDED

❑ DRIED FLOWERS AND NATURALS
❑ BIRCH BRANCHES
❑ SHEET MOSS
❑ CONTAINER
❑ PLASTIC FOAM BLOCK AND BALL

Topiary Treatments

To make the topiary shown, use dried roses, baby's breath, dried cockscomb, dried lemon leaves, sheet moss and birch branch. Other choices follow.

SUGGESTED CHOICES FOR COVERINGS

COUNTRY	FESTIVE	UNIQUE
Fresh autumn leaves	Red rosebuds	Garlic bulbs
Silk flowers	Pinecones	Dyed pistachios
Dried rose petals	Holly berries & leaves	Dried fruit
Strawflowers	Fresh cranberries	Green sheet moss
Amaranthus	Small ornamental balls	Nigella pods
Bachelor's buttons	Spruce greens	Nuts in shells
Hydrangea florets	Boxwood leaves	Artificial fruit
Delphinium	Bright silk flowers	Popcorn

HOW TO MAKE THE DRIED FLOWER TABLETOP TOPIARY

1 Glue a sheet of moss around plastic foam ball, centering it on top and wrapping around to the bottom. Fill any blank spaces with extra moss, leaving a small space at the bottom of the ball for stick.

2 Push the ball firmly onto the top of the stick until it is inserted about halfway into the plastic foam. Apply glue to the top of the stick where it joins the plastic foam to hold it in place.

3 Use scissors to cut shallow arcs into the bases of several lemon leaves. This will make them conform to the shape of the plastic foam ball and they will be easier to glue on.

HANDY HINTS

Use fresh baby's breath instead of the very fragile dried version. Allow the blossoms to dry naturally in the topiary arrangement. The fresh blossoms are easier to work with and will not fall apart with handling.

If the topiary is top-heavy, use clay to fill the base and insert branch into it.

4 Apply glue to the trimmed edge of a large leaf and stick it onto lower portion of ball. Hold until adhered. Continue adding leaves, using larger leaves on the bottom and smaller ones on top.

5 Glue roses and cockscomb among the lemon leaves. Hold each in place until adhered. Continue adding flowers until the topiary is filled out.

6 Take several baby's breath blossoms and twist an 8-inch piece of wire around stems. Stick into ball among flowers. Continue until topiary looks full and lush.

7 Glue another sheet of moss to the base to cover the plastic foam in the container. Cut or tear small pieces of the moss to fill out empty spaces.

QUICK FIX

If you can't find birch branches at the local florist, pick up some birch bark shavings instead. They come in very thin layers that can be glued onto a plain branch or dowel to duplicate the look of a birch branch.

Bright Ideas: Specialty Arrangements

Gather fruits, nuts, spices and berries for a wintry accent, or arrange dried flowers and grasses in a summery ensemble.

Colorful & Festive

Combine nature's rich berry reds and warm nutty browns with an array of dried lemon leaves for a lasting holiday topiary that's cause for celebration.

• Use a gleaming golden container as the base for this topiary to contrast with the rustic twisted quality of the branch.

• Glue on lemon leaves and then fill in spaces with dried orange slices and nuts in their shells.

• Add clusters of red pepper berries and artfully insert whole cinnamon sticks.

• Decorate the base with berries, cinnamon and a golden bow.

A Loose Interpretation

For a casual, open arrangement, use light-colored wildflowers and neutral grasses. To avoid symmetry, vary the length and height of the items.

• Use a sturdy but decorative rectangular terra-cotta pot.

• Randomly insert or glue rye, curly willow, pepper grass and statice into place.

• Add pepper berries, lavender and cockscomb for color.

• Top the topiary base with sheet moss, reindeer moss and extra dried flowers.

EASY AND ELEGANT FLORAL FRAMES

Colorful dried flowers add style and distinction to a plain frame.

BEFORE YOU BEGIN

You can really dress up a plain wooden frame! Make it glamorous by gilding it with gold paint before adding the flowers.

Any type of frame can be decorated with dried flowers. A plain wooden frame has a natural and informal look, while a gold frame is more elegant.

Use a combination of paints for a quick and easy way to add a special touch to a plain frame. Standard decorative painting techniques such as marbling, ragging and sponging can all be used to make unique frames.

Once the frame has been painted, decorate the front with dried flowers that complement the color and material of the frame.

To make a gold frame, clean and dry the surface. Then apply an even coat of black enamel paint to provide a glossy base for the gold paint. Allow to dry.

Use a soft, dry cloth to rub a layer of light gold acrylic paint all over the frame. Apply the paint liberally, but do not worry about uniformity. Allow to dry.

TOOL NEEDED
❏ GLUE GUN AND GLUE STICKS

MATERIALS NEEDED
❏ FRAME
❏ DRIED LEMON LEAVES
❏ 2 BUNCHES DRIED WHITE AND BLUE DELPHINIUM
❏ 1 BUNCH DRIED SALVIA
❏ 1 BUNCH DRIED ROSES

Golden Ideas

Try these alternative ways to add a golden glow to picture frames:

• Apply gold leaf sheets to the frame using special gold leaf adhesive. This is particularly effective on frames which feature raised detailing.
• Use a small decorative stamp to apply metallic gold accents on a flat frame. For the best effect, paint the frame in a dark color first.

HOW TO MAKE EASY AND ELEGANT FLORAL FRAMES

1 Once frame is dry, apply glue to ends and backs of lemon leaves. Position leaves along upper left corner and lower right corner to create a base for flowers. Overlap leaves to create a lush look.

2 Working on one corner at a time, apply glue to ends of blue delphinium stems. Tuck stems under lemon leaves so that stems are not visible and delphinium flowers radiate out from corner.

HANDY HINTS

Instead of leaves for the base of the display, cut a piece of florist's foam to fit the corner of the frame. Glue the foam in place and then insert the stems.

TAKE NOTE

Hot glue dries very quickly. Make sure the delicate flowers are positioned exactly the way you want before fixing them in place.

3 Intersperse white delphinium and salvia flowers between leaves and blue delphinium for color and balance. Make sure stems are positioned correctly before gluing into place.

4 Finish display by filling in open areas with yellow roses for an additional splash of color. Remove stems from roses and apply glue directly to underside of flower. Make sure roses are grouped closely enough to cover any visible delphinium stems.

Bright Ideas: Specialty Frames

Add the delicate beauty of roses or the color and texture of amaranths to create one-of-a-kind frames.

Floral Crown

Soothing, shades of blue, green, pink and purple dried flowers complement this washed green frame.

• Completely cover the upper edge of a mid-sized frame with a pretty mix of dried flowers. Use dark green oregano leaves as the base, gluing them directly onto the frame.

• Add short stems of amaranth as a contrast to the oregano. Fill in with pale blue hydrangea blossoms and purple salvia.

Rose Gallery

Romantic miniature rosebuds in shades of pink, peach and yellow add a Victorian feeling to this mini gallery.

• Attach the flowers to the frames in a variety of different arrangements to create an eye-catching tabletop display.

• Remove the stems and glue the rosebuds directly to the frame. Attach delphinium and baby's breath to add color and fill in any open areas. Add some leaves for green contrast.

• Use pretty wired ribbon bows to add a delicate accent to the corner of some of the frames.

Easy Natural Vine Wreath

Simple treasures from your yard and garden help create this one-of-a-kind but absolutely gorgeous and graceful vine wreath.

BEFORE YOU BEGIN

This wreath is meant to be loosely wrapped with extending vine as it naturally occurs. Take advantage of the natural elements as they happen, and use varying diameters of vine. Keep the wreath open and airy. The goal is not to emulate the thick, heavy-looking purchased wreaths. Embellishments should be natural elements from your yard or woods. The dried flower blossoms should be ones with larger heads such as hydrangeas or sunflowers. Many large blossoms, such as hydrangeas, can be easily air-dried in a vase. The blossoms will be the focal point, and the backdrop for them can be evergreen or cedar sprigs with or without berries. Be cautious with berries such as mistletoe, making sure they are not toxic to pets or small children. If you choose to wire the large blossoms on, they can be changed, either to refresh the look or to use silk poinsettia blossoms for a holiday theme.

The wreath should be from 18 inches to 24 inches in diameter. Using natural elements harvested from the yard or woods, the cost is only a few dollars. The project takes less than an hour.

1 Cut at least three lengths of wire to have ready to wrap the vines to secure them. Take a length of vine and loop into a circle of desired size. Hold securely at top of loop and keep adding lengths of vine until the wreath is desired density. Using a cut length of wire, wrap top of wreath securely. Decide on the two other focal points, besides the top, which will have a bow, and wire the vines loosely together at those points. The three focal points should form an imaginary irregular triangle. Tuck in any vines that are out of control and not part of the design.

2 Place evergreen or cedar sprigs at the lower two focal points. Usually it is best to make one design area more dominant by using larger or more elements. When satisfied with the placement, wire sprigs in place, wiring from front to back. Wrap wire securely and tuck end out of the way. Make sure to also wire the tips of the sprigs to hold them in place, making sure to conceal these wires.

3 Hydrangeas are very fragile. They can be wired using florist's wire along the 1½-inch stem and wrapping with florist's tape and wiring them into the wreath, or they can be glued with a glue gun from the back side. Make a raffia bow about 12 to 14 inches wide and wire to top of wreath. Wrap raffia around center of bow and wreath to form knot for bow. On the back, make a wire loop to hang wreath.

Miniature Flowering Box Gardens

Bring the outdoors inside with mini versions of a summer garden.

BEFORE YOU BEGIN

How you prepare the box before planting your mini garden is very important. Take these preparatory steps to prevent the box from becoming stained or damaged.

Choose a sturdy box with a solid bottom. Make sure the sides meet squarely at the corners so that water and soil don't leak out. Check the outside of the box for nails, splinters and other potentially dangerous protrusions.

Consider lining the sides and bottom of the box with moss, dead leaves or other dried natural materials if you are concerned that the plastic will show through. This will also provide an additional barrier against moisture.

Using a paintbrush, paint the inside of the box with wood sealant or waterproof varnish; let dry. For extra protection, paint the outside of the box as well. If you prefer a bright, colorful box instead of one with a natural finish, substitute waterproof paint for the varnish.

To protect the box from moisture and the surface on which it is placed from leakage, lay a plastic trash bag over the box and press it flat on the bottom and into the side. Let the edges hang over the top of the box.

TOOLS NEEDED

❏ Scissors
❏ Paintbrush
❏ trowel

MATERIALS NEEDED

❏ Wooden box
❏ Waterproof sealer
❏ Potting soil
❏ Assorted flowering plants
❏ Grass seeds
❏ Plastic trash bag

Which Box?

Here are some ideas on boxes to use for your mini gardens.

• Wooden planters made from aged wood with a natural finish create a rustic look. Shipping crates, wine boxes and durable fruit baskets with solid bottoms also have rustic appeal.
• Plastic boxes with deep sides are colorful and contemporary.
• Strong wicker baskets will also work well. Be sure to hide the plastic liner with moss or dead leaves.

HOW TO MAKE MINIATURE FLOWERING BOX GARDENS

1 Fill a lined box with potting soil, leaving a 1-inch gap at top of box. Sprinkle grass seeds on top, and cover with a thin layer of soil. Water well and place in a sunny spot. Grass will begin to grow in seven to 10 days.

2 Once grass has grown to at least 4 inches long, use liner to help you remove it from box in one clump. Working on top of liner, gently separate grass into smaller clumps using fingers or a butter knife.

3 Line planter with fresh plastic and fill with soil to within 1 inch of top. Dig a hole in middle of soil and add a seasonal flowering plant. Gently dig holes around plant, being careful not to damage roots; add small clumps of grass. Carefully pat down soil around plant and grass to secure.

HANDY HINTS

In darker rooms, use mini box gardens as a colorful, decorative accessory for special occasions. But move them to sunnier spots for everyday storage.

4 Once plants are pleasingly arranged in planter, use scissors to cut liner so that it is level with top of box. Place box on a table or windowsill that receives appropriate amount of light for flowering plant. Water regularly; feed during spring and summer months. If grass grows too long, use a sharp pair of scissors to trim it to desired length. Properly cared for, box garden should last indefinitely.

Bright Ideas: Flower Box Variations

The long, wispy blades of grass offer a sharp contrast to the curvy leaves and vibrant buds of flowering plants.

Window Box Beauty

A mini box garden on an inside windowsill is a fun twist on traditional outdoor window boxes.

• A long, rectangular box not only fills up window space, but also provides enough room to add an assortment of beautiful flowering plants.

• Use different varieties of flowering plants in the same color families to create continuity within your mini box garden.

• Add depth to the display by putting taller plants at the back of the box.

Box of Surprises

A small square box of flowers and grass placed on the edge of a corner table adds a visual surprise to the decor.

• Choose a flowering plant in a bold, brilliant color to contrast a neutral decorating scheme. These vibrant red begonias are attention-grabbing and enliven their muted surroundings with a splash of bright color.

• The textures of the grass and the foliage of the plant also create visual interest.

• The various shades of green in the leaves also provide a colorful background for the red begonias.

TABLETOP TREE ARRANGEMENTS

Create your own personal indoor forest with these pretty little "trees."

BEFORE YOU BEGIN

A miniature tree makes a delightful and aromatic decoration for any time of year. To create your very own mini forest, group together several trees made from different greens.

Preparing the base and greens properly is critical. Shape the tree base from a block of florist's foam. Soak the block in water overnight, then use a sharp knife to cut and shape the foam into the shape of a pyramid.

Select a container that is proportional to the size of the tree—a plastic saucer would work well. Make sure the foam fits snugly.

To obtain the sprigs needed to create a mini tree, use sharp florist's scissors to cut the tips from fresh branches. Cut a variety of lengths so the arrangement will have an authentic tree shape. Choose from a variety of different evergreens to make your tree, including holly, boxwood, pine, spruce, juniper or cypress. Leave berries in place for an even more realistic tree.

To make shorter sprigs easier to position in the foam, wire the bottom of the stems to 2-inch florist's picks. If the pick has no wire, use a piece of thin florist's wire to join the pick and sprig together.

To help your tree last longer, add water to the bottom of the saucer and keep the arrangement away from direct sunlight. Some evergreens such as princess pine, boxwood and ivy will dry naturally over time and still maintain their fresh, green color. Other evergreens can be preserved easily with glycerin to create a miniature tree that will last for years.

TOOLS NEEDED

❏ CRAFT KNIFE
❏ FLORIST'S SCISSORS

MATERIALS NEEDED

❏ EVERGREEN SPRIGS
❏ FLORIST'S FOAM
❏ SMALL TERRA-COTTA POT
❏ FLORIST'S WIRE
❏ FLORIST'S PICKS

HOW TO MAKE TABLETOP TREE ARRANGEMENTS

1 Soak block of florist's foam in water overnight. Measure width and depth of container and mark bottom of foam to fit snugly inside. Use a sharp craft knife to carve foam into cone shape (*Before You Begin*).

2 Cut tips off evergreen branches to create short sprigs ranging in length from 1 to 6 inches. To condition, use a sharp knife to scrape off bark from bottom of stems, then cut them diagonally and slit up middle.

3 Starting at bottom with longest sprigs, insert stems or picks into foam. Point sprigs slightly downward to create a realistic tree shape. Work upward using increasingly shorter sprigs.

HANDY HINTS

If florist's foam crumbles, wrap it in fine mesh chicken wire about 1 foot wide. Strong stems like boxwood do not need to be wired to picks.

4 Continue inserting sprigs until foam is completely covered. Use florist's scissors to prune and shape tree into a perfect cone shape—step back and check the shape. Keep foam well watered to extend life of arrangement.

DOLLAR SENSE

Use branches from the trees and shrubs around your house to make your mini tree. This way, when sprigs start to look wilted, they can be replaced with fresh ones from outside.

Bright Ideas: "Special Trees"

Add fruit, flowers and other decorations to your tree to create a festive arrangement that takes up minimal space on a table or windowsill.

Fruitful Tree

Add an assortment of fruit and flowers along with a beautiful silk ribbon to an arrangement of fresh juniper sprigs to create a glorious centerpiece.
• Shape florist's foam into a cone shape and insert juniper sprigs as described in steps.
• Tie a wire-edged ribbon into a long-tailed bow. Wire the bow in place and weave the tails through the sprigs.
• Glue plastic fruit or use florist's picks to insert fresh fruit into the arrangement.
• Insert fresh or dried flowers into the foam so they nestle among the juniper sprigs.

Happy Holly-days

Deck your holiday table with a miniature Christmas tree made from holly branches, ornaments and beads.
• Use holly to cover a cone-shaped piece of foam as described in steps.
• Wire heavy ornaments to florist's picks and insert them into the foam. Hang lighter ornaments directly from the sprigs. Add a treetop ornament at the pinnacle as the finishing touch.
• Weave red and gold beads through the branches of the tree.
• Complete the display by placing miniature gifts beneath the tree.

WINDOWSILL GARDEN BOXES

Ceramic tiles add a special touch to a windowsill box.

BEFORE YOU BEGIN

The enormous selection of ceramic tiles available makes it easy to construct a unique windowsill box. Create a sill box and tile design that is personalized for your window.

Planning the tile placement is a critical step. The windowsill size will provide an estimate of how big the box should be, but the exact size depends on the dimensions of the tiles as well as the tile pattern.

Measure the depth and width of the windowsill to ensure the box will fit. Lay the selected ceramic tiles on a table or other durable surface. Arrange tiles to create the desired pattern for the front, back and end pieces. Allow a slight space, about $\frac{1}{8}$ inch, for grout between the tiles.

Measure the total length of the tiles, then add two times the thickness of a tile to the side measurements. To ensure fit, make sure the dimensions are smaller than those of the windowsill.

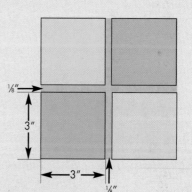

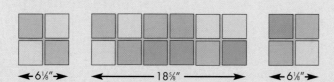

6⅛"   18⅝"   6⅛"

Cutting the Plywood

Here's how to cut the plywood for your windowsill garden box.

• For the ends of the box, cut two pieces of pine to the dimensions of the tile pattern design, minus 1 inch in width and $\frac{1}{2}$ inch in height.
• For the front and back, cut two pieces of pine according to pattern measurements, minus $\frac{1}{2}$ inch in height and $\frac{1}{2}$ inch in width. This will allow the box's front and back tiles to overlap the ends of the side tiles.
• Once all four sides are nailed together, measure the inside of the box to determine the dimensions of the bottom piece.

HOW TO MAKE A WINDOWSILL GARDEN BOX

1 Apply carpenter's glue to the side edges of both end pieces. Attach the front and back pieces to the end pieces with the edges flush. Secure the pieces together with several #4 finishing nails.

2 Insert the bottom piece inside the box. Hammer nails through each side directly into the bottom piece, being careful that the pieces stay properly aligned. Paint or stain the inside of the box, if desired.

3 Use a ruler and pencil to mark the tile pattern directly onto the box according to layout. Remember that the tiles will extend beyond the wood and to allow room between the tiles for grout (*Before You Begin*).

HANDY HINTS

Since decorative tiles are quite expensive, a windowsill box is an ideal way to display beautiful tiles with minimal expense. Resilient vinyl tiles are less expensive than ceramic tiles and make a worthy substitute. Since most resilient tiles feature a sticky back, they eliminate the need for glue and grout.

4 Glue tiles to the two ends of the window box first. Apply two or three drops of hot glue to the back of a tile and quickly apply it to the box. (Tile adhesive, which dries more slowly than glue, can also be used.)

5 Apply the remaining tiles to the front and the back of the box in a similar manner. However, be sure to position the front and back tiles to cover the edges of the tiles on the end pieces.

6 Using a sponge, apply grout to the box, one side at a time, working the grout into the seams. Use a clean sponge to wipe away excess grout. Rinse the sponge and repeat several times. Glue a medallion to the front of the box, if desired. Wait a full day to allow grout to dry, then line the inside of the windowsill box with plastic and fill with soil and plants. Set on windowsill.

Bright Ideas: Window Box Style

Design your own unique window boxes with interesting tiles. Look for tiles with textures and colorful patterns.

Simple Sophistication

The beauty of natural tile is enhanced with sculpted border tiles and fresh flowers to create a romantic effect.
• Many tiles are sold with coordinating or border tiles. From intricate, patterned tiles to simple solid-colored tiles, it is easy to design all kinds of effects, from earthy to elegant.
• Select the sculpted tile first, since this will set the mood of the window box.
• Make sure the size of the border and base tiles combined is in proportion to the size of the window.

Window Harvest

Hand-painted ceramic tiles add a touch of wonderful freshness to a windowsill box full of green herbs.
• Glue half-rounded tiles along the top edges to finish the box.
• If the hand-painted tiles prove too expensive, use plain white tiles on the back of the box that will not be seen.
• To keep the box clean and neat, simply plant the herbs in small terra-cotta pots that fit inside the windowsill box.
• Herbs are easy to grow in a small spot like a window box and are convenient to have on hand for a special garnish.

GARDEN THEME DECORATOR PILLOWS

Use your favorite garden stamps to create a decorator pillow with a garden theme. Complement your decorator pillow with other pillows made from the classic pinwheel quilt square.

BEFORE YOU BEGIN

You have all those garden stamps that you bought to make special cards for friends and relatives. Now you can put them to good use again to stamp an outline on a fabric square, hand stitch the picture with embroidery floss, and then construct a border and back to form the cover for a pillow. Vary the size of the pillow to add interest. Smaller pillows can accommodate one stamp and larger pillows can use more than one stamp.

Search your favorite garden books to find interesting sayings to add to the pictures. Select some of the sayings with a gift theme in mind so you can give your own hand-made pillows for birthdays and holidays. Hand stitch a child's name on the pillow and use it to decorate their room or hang from their doorknob to announce whose room it is. Embellish the pillow with buttons, wire, raffia, fabric bows and your own personal favorites to create a pillow to adorn a shelf, bench or chair or create a wall decoration to hang on a shelf peg. Group your hand-stitched pillow with other classic quilt square pillows in complementary colors to decorate larger areas.

TOOLS NEEDED

- ❏ SCISSORS
- ❏ NEEDLES
- ❏ SEWING MACHINE
- ❏ CUTTING MAT
- ❏ ROTARY CUTTER
- ❏ CUTTING RULER
- ❏ IRON
- ❏ GARDEN STAMPS
- ❏ EMBROIDERY HOOP

MATERIALS NEEDED

- ❏ LIGHT MUSLIN OR TEA-STAINED FABRIC
- ❏ ABOUT ½ YARD OF TWO TO THREE COMPLEMENTARY FABRICS (ONE LIGHT, ONE OR TWO DARK)
- ❏ LIGHT THREAD FOR SEWING MACHINE
- ❏ EMBROIDERY FLOSS
- ❏ WASHABLE INK PAD
- ❏ FIBERFILL

HOW TO MAKE A HAND-STITCHED PILLOW

1 From light muslin or tea-stained fabric, and using a rotary cutter, mat and cutting ruler, cut a square or rectangle that is big enough to accommodate the stamp(s) and also allow a $\frac{1}{4}$-inch seam allowance. Size may vary depending upon stamp or grouping. If using your favorite saying, ensure that the size is big enough to accommodate lettering that is easily readable. Garden verses can be added without a stamp by simply writing the letters on the fabric in washable-ink pen. Stamp the picture or verse on the fabric using washable ink. If you stamp the picture on crooked, just rinse the ink out by running warm water over it, press slightly dry in a towel, press and try again.

2 From one of the complementary fabrics, cut one or two 2-inch strips to use for a border. The number of border pieces will depend on the size of the muslin square.

3 Sew 2-inch border to the top and bottom of the stamped square using a $\frac{1}{4}$-inch seam allowance. Trim ends of border even with the sides. Press seams to the outside. Then sew 2-inch border to the left and right of the stamped square using a $\frac{1}{4}$-inch seam allowance. Trim ends of border to form a square or rectangle. Press seams to the outside. *Optional:* A second border in another complementary fabric may also be added. Cut a $2\frac{1}{2}$- or 3-inch border and sew to the first border starting at the top and bottom and then moving to the left and right of the first border.

4 Using embroidery floss and embroidery hoop, hand stitch the outline of the stamp using a backstitch. If the stamp has a colored picture on the back, use the stamp back to help select the color of the floss. When needed, use a French knot or satin stitch. When all stitching is complete, rinse the fabric square to remove any ink that may be showing. Press the square with the seam allowances to the outside.

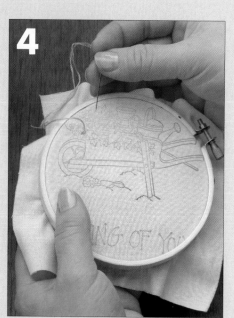

5 Cut an $8\frac{1}{4}$-inch strip from the same fabric as the first border. Cut the strip into $8\frac{1}{4}$-inch squares. Layer the hand-stitched square over the fabric square, matching the corners and sides and with right sides together. Stitch front to back on all sides using a $\frac{1}{4}$-inch seam allowance leaving a small opening to turn and stuff the pillow. Trim corners and turn inside out. Press.

6 Stuff the pillow cover with fiberfill or a pillow form. Slip stitch the opening closed using a blanket stitch. Attach a gift tag if it will be used for a gift.

HANDY HINTS

Using the rotary cutting tools really makes this process go quickly and results in well-proportioned squares.

It is great to have several smaller pillows made ahead of time to give for special occasions.

TAKE NOTE

When writing on the pillow, be sure to use a guide so that the lettering stays straight and centered on the square. It may even help to write the words out on paper first until you get the letter size and spacing correct.

Select stamps that have a large outline pattern rather than ones that are very detailed. This simplifies the hand stitching and results in more crisp pictures.

HOW TO MAKE A PINWHEEL QUILT SQUARE

1 From one of the light-colored fabrics, and using a rotary cutter, mat and cutting ruler, cut a 4⁷/₈-inch strip of fabric. Cut the same width strip from the dark fabric also. Put the two colored fabrics right sides together and cut the strips into 4⁷/₈-inch squares. Using a pen, draw a straight line from one diagonal corner to the other.

2 Sew a seam ¹/₄ inch from either side of the line. Cut the square into two triangles by cutting on the diagonal line.

3 Press the seam toward the darker fabric to form a square.

4 Arrange four of the squares in a pinwheel pattern. Sew the top left square to the top right square. Sew the bottom right square to the bottom left square. Press the top two squares with the seam toward the right side of the rectangle. Press the bottom two squares with the seam toward the left side of the rectangle. Sew the top squares to the bottom squares, matching the center seams. Press the seam toward the bottom squares. Cut one or two 2-inch strips from the darker fabric.

5 Sew 2-inch border to the top and bottom of the quilt square using a ¹/₄-inch seam allowance. Trim ends of border. Press seams to the outside. Then sew 2-inch border to the left and right of the quilt square using a ¹/₄-inch seam allowance. Trim ends of border to form a square or rectangle. Press seams to the outside. Cut 12-inch square from border fabric. Layer the quilt square over the fabric square, matching the corners and sides and with right sides together. Stitch front to back on all sides using a ¹/₄-inch seam allowance leaving a small opening to turn and stuff the pillow.

6 Trim corners and turn inside out. Press. Fill using fiberfill or a pillow form. Slip stitch the opening.

HANDY HINTS

Be sure to cut several strips and then several squares at one time so that you can sew the pieces together in assembly fashion and create several smaller squares at a time. This helps to speed the process along.

TAKE NOTE

When selecting your favorite garden sayings, it is fun to stitch the name of the author at the bottom of the saying, especially if the author is well known or from another era. It adds a nice historical touch to the craft.

HANDY HINTS

Omit fiberfill and simply slip stitch the opening. Attach a small wooden dowel to the top back using a slip stitch. Use quilt square as a wall hanging.

OUTDOOR

You can decorate your garden, patio, doors, entryways and windows with garden themes! What better way to celebrate the garden, than doing it outdoors where all the excitement starts in the first place? From a decorative mini-birdbath to twinkling garden lights, and from pretty birdhouses to wind chimes, a very special trellis and so much more, these ideas and instructions will help you make your home's outdoor greeting and living areas about as inviting and friendly as you can imagine.

COPPER PIPE TRELLIS

Copper pipe offers a wonderful contrast to the greenery of any garden or patio. It is also a fast and easy way to customize a trellis to your specific gardening needs. Create a mini- or full-sized trellis with these plans!

BEFORE YOU BEGIN

Through the years the copper can change to a rich patina or it can be polished for a shiny look. This mini-trellis (left) works well in a patio pot, to add support for a climbing plant, such as a clematis or morning glory. It will fit a standard 16-inch clay pot with sloping sides or any planter or container with vertical sides that measure more than 14 inches. The larger version can by used as a traditional trellis, next to a fence or wall. Dimensions and layout are given for both and the assembly is the same. Dimensions best utilize the 10-foot length of pipe, but the design can be expanded both vertically and horizontally, as desired. If expanding the size of the mini-trellis, another copper pipe length would need to be purchased.

The finished dimensions for the mini-trellis are $12\frac{1}{2}$ inches wide by $30\frac{1}{2}$ inches high with about 24 inches above the dirt. It takes about $1\frac{1}{2}$ hours to cut and assemble plus drying time. The cost of the materials is about $10.00. The finished dimensions for the full-sized trellis are 33 inches wide by 66 inches high with about 60 inches above the ground. It takes about $2\frac{1}{2}$ hours to cut and assemble plus drying time. The cost is about $35.00. All materials can be purchased at a local home improvement store or hardware store. Salvage copper also can be used.

TOOLS NEEDED

MINI-TRELLIS
- ❏ POLYURETHANE GLUE (OR ANY GLUE RECOMMENDED FOR METALS)
- ❏ TUBE CUTTER OR HACKSAW WITH BLADE FOR CUTTING METAL

FULL-SIZED TRELLIS
- ❏ POLYURETHANE GLUE
- ❏ TUBE CUTTER OR HACKSAW WITH BLADE FOR CUTTING METAL
- ❏ SHOULDER OR SQUARE BEND SCREW HOOK—IF NEEDED

MATERIALS NEEDED

MINI-TRELLIS
- ❏ 10-FOOT LENGTH OF $\frac{1}{2}$-INCH RIGID COPPER PIPE
- ❏ ELEVEN $\frac{1}{2}$-INCH COPPER TEE'S
- ❏ TWO $\frac{1}{2}$-INCH COPPER ELBOWS (CORNERS)

FULL-SIZED TRELLIS
- ❏ THREE 10-FOOT LENGTHS OF $\frac{3}{4}$-INCH RIGID COPPER PIPE
- ❏ TWENTY $\frac{3}{4}$-INCH COPPER TEE'S
- ❏ TWO $\frac{3}{4}$-INCH COPPER ELBOW (CORNER) JOINTS

HOW TO MAKE A MINI-TRELLIS

1 Mark the cutting line with masking tape, for the following lengths: eight at 7½ inches (for vertical pieces); eight at 2¼ inches (for internal horizontal pieces); two at about 12 inches (for lower side vertical pieces); two at 5 inches (for top horizontal pieces).

2 Cut pipe with tube cutter or hack saw. When using the hack saw place pipe in a vice, however do not tighten too much as it will dent the pipe. The pipe cutter is cleaner and easier to use. It helps to use rubber gloves or rubberized garden gloves to help grip the pipe and also to avoid getting residue from the pipe on hands.

3 Assemble the pieces as shown in the layout. Work on a surface that is covered with paper to protect it and large enough to lay the entire project flat. If making the full-sized trellis, it may mean working on the floor. This will keep it flat while assembling and while drying if it is glued. Work from the inside joints out. The joints will be a bit tight which is fine. If they are tight gluing is not necessary. The project does not have to be made waterproof.

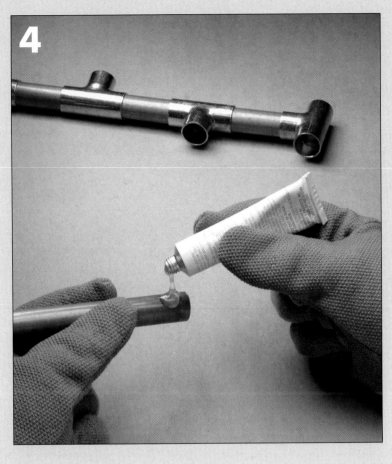

4 When satisfied with the assembly, glue if necessary. Use glue recommended for metals. Use very little glue and put it on the end and outside of pipe to be inserted. Be sure to insert pipe all the way and square it up, by setting it on the work surface. While drying keep the project lying flat and follow the drying instructions on the product. Polish, if desired, with a copper cleaner or leave as is. Place into the pot with bottom pipes going into the soil about 4 to 5 inches.

HOW TO MAKE A FULL-SIZED TRELLIS

5 Mark copper pipe as in step 1 with masking tape in the following lengths: fourteen at 11 inches (for vertical pieces); sixteen at 7 inches (for internal horizontal pieces); two at 18 inches (for lower side vertical pieces); three at 15 inches (for top horizontal pieces and bottom center vertical piece). Cut as in step 2. Assemble the pieces as shown in this layout, following information in step 3.

6 Polish, if desired, as in step 4. Place along wall or fence with bottom pipes going into the soil about 6 inches. Add support by attaching the trellis on both sides near the top to the wall or fence, using a shoulder or square bend screw hook. Drill a pilot hole if necessary.

HANDY HINTS

Add other copper shapes and designs by wiring them onto the trellis with copper wire or hanging them with monofilament fishing line.

TAKE NOTE

Copper can be made into patina faster with chemicals that cause this reaction. The chemicals are available at craft stores and paint centers.

Decorative Mini-Birdbath

This birdbath will look unique, sitting on a patio table or bench. Fill it with water and put floating candles or flower blossoms in it.

BEFORE YOU BEGIN

Made from natural elements, it will blend into the outdoors on a patio or porch or even in a garden. Make three mini-birdbaths in three different sizes and group them together. Use pebbles or stones, about $1/2$ to 1 inch in diameter. These may be from the yard or buy them at a nursery or landscape company. They usually will sell them by the bucket. Do not use polished stones from a craft store as they will not permanently adhere to the adhesive. Other natural elements can be used for this project, such as sea glass for lining the saucer and sea grass rope wound around the base.

This project takes a couple of hours to do, but the drying time for the adhesive is 24 hours and is necessary to securely adhere the stones. The birdbath can be made smaller or larger than the example given. For the 10-inch birdbath, the cost is about $9.00.

MATERIALS NEEDED

❑ PRE-MIX ADHESIVE AND GROUT—SANDED
❑ STONES—NO LARGER THAN $1/2$ TO 1 INCH—IN VARIOUS SHAPES AND COLORS
❑ 10-INCH CLAY SAUCER
❑ 4-INCH CLAY ROSE POT (THE ROSE POT IS A BIT TALLER THAN A STANDARD 4-INCH POT)
❑ 15 FEET OF STRAIGHT WILLOW TWIGS—$1/4$ TO $1/2$ INCH IN DIAMETER
❑ COPPER WIRE—18 GAUGE
❑ ACRYLIC LATEX CAULK—CLEAR

TOOLS NEEDED

❑ GLUE GUN
❑ WIRE CUTTER

HOW TO MAKE A DECORATIVE MINI-BIRDBATH

1 Wash stones well so that no sand is left on them. Let them dry. Put masking tape around wall of saucer about $1/4$ inch from bottom to protect from adhesive.

HANDY HINTS

Use **broken tile** or broken china plates instead of the stones to line the bottom of the saucers for the birdbath.

2 Using a putty knife, spread the bottom of clay saucer with about $1/8$ inch of adhesive. Lay out stones on work surface, finding the most level side for each stone. Start laying the stones in the adhesive, pushing them gently into the adhesive. Push adhesive around the stones a bit to help hold it in place. Adding extra adhesive to the bottom of the stone before putting it in will also help. Vary the size, color and shape of stones for an attractive design. Be sure to wash any tools used and remove any adhesive in areas where it is not wanted, because once it starts drying it can-not be removed. Let dry for 24 hours.

3 To cover the clay rose pot, cut twigs slightly less than the height of pot, in this case 5½ inches. Measure around the outside of pot at largest part, in this case 14 inches. Line twigs up on flat surface, placing the tapering end toward the top. Cut two pieces of copper wire about twice the measurement around the pot and twist ends together at one end. Start wrapping or weaving the wire around the twigs, about 1 inch from bottom. Occasionally put in a shorter twig to create more tapering. When this measures about 2 inches less than pot measurement, stop.

4 Place twigs around upside-down pot. Temporarily twist wire together to hold in place. Put a rubber band around twigs toward the top (actually the bottom) of pot to hold everything in place. Adjust twigs evenly. Finish putting in final twigs to complete the design. Twist wires securely together, trim wire and tuck ends behind twigs.

5 With glue gun, glue top of twigs in place. Remove rubber band and base is done.

6 Put a substantial bead of clear latex caulk around top of base (actually bottom of the pot). Center saucer over the base and place securely on base. Let dry as recommended by manufacturer.

TAKE NOTE

For display purposes, make three mini birdbaths in varying sizes and cluster them together, or use them in descending order as bases for a cascading water fountain.

GARDEN LIGHT, GARDEN BRIGHT

Enjoy the night in the garden with these beautiful, bright lights.

BEFORE YOU BEGIN

Using empty glass jars, wire and beads you can create a colorful lantern. Light a path, have an evening lantern parade, make a circle of light on a table for outdoor dining. Everyone in the family can enjoy and join in on this project!

1 Begin with a clean jar. Measure wire to wrap around the neck of the jar and loop over the top to form a handle for carrying; add an extra 4 inches to the length for attaching wire.

2 Wrap wire around the neck of the jar, leaving an extra 2 inches on one side for finishing beads. Twist wire together with small pliers, securing it around the jar's neck. Loop the wire over the top to make a handle shape. The handle height can vary, keeping in mind the heat of the candle inside. Measure enough wire to meet the end of the twisted wire at the neck of the jar, then add an extra 2 inches for finishing beads. Using wire cutter, cut wire, leaving cut end free to string beads.

3 String beads onto open end of the wire. Think creatively of how to use colors, sizes and shapes. Cover wire with beads, leaving several inches of extra empty space, letting beads separate at the top curve of the handle for easy carrying. Finish beading, leaving 2 inches of wire to secure to jar neck wire. Loop wire onto the jar neck wire and twist with small pliers to secure, making sure the wire is firmly fitted to the neck. Finish beading ends of wire. To keep beads in place, crimp bottom $1/2$ inch of wired ends into a small circle using small pliers. For added interest, other pieces of wire can be measured, twisted, beaded and attached to main beaded wire.

4 Place a tea light in each jar, light and carry off to brighten the night!

TOOLS NEEDED
❏ SMALL PLIERS
❏ WIRE CUTTER

MATERIALS NEEDED
❏ GLASS JARS, CANNING JARS, ANY EMPTY FOOD JARS THAT ARE WIDE ENOUGH TO PLACE A TEA LIGHT CANDLE INSIDE. SIZES AND SHAPES CAN VARY AND WILL ADD EXTRA INTEREST.
❏ WIRE, 18-20 GAUGE
❏ BEADS—MANY COLORS, SIZES, SHAPES, AND VARIETIES
❏ TEA LIGHTS

Fairy Garden

For the young and the young of heart: A small garden of enchantment, and a home to fairies, elves and all who believe in magic fantasy.

BEFORE YOU BEGIN

Find a small spot in your garden and begin thinking small. Plantings in this miniature garden can include lily of the valley, forget-me-nots, sweet woodruff, primrose, heather, creeping phlox, violets, pansies, nasturtium, creeping thyme, Queen Anne's lace, miniature roses, ferns and hostas. Change objects by thinking small; a thimble becomes a garden flowerpot, a seashell becomes a birdbath, a mirror becomes a pond, a pinecone becomes a tree. In this fairy garden the small ideas are big and imaginative, adding fun and inspiration to your whole garden.

TOOLS NEEDED

❏ CLIPPERS
❏ FLORIST'S WIRE
❏ SMALL PLIERS
❏ GLUE GUN
❏ X-ACTO KNIFE

MATERIALS NEEDED

❏ STICKS
❏ LEAVES
❏ REINDEER MOSS
❏ TREE BARK
❏ PINECONES
❏ FLAGSTONE OR SMALL ROCKS
❏ SEASHELLS
❏ SMALL MIRROR
❏ GLITTER

HOW TO MAKE A FAIRY GARDEN

HANDY HINTS

Birch tree bark works well as a house form for this project.

1 Begin by choosing your house form. A rounded tree bark works well and is easy to cut into. Sticks can also be used to make a square house form. For a rounded form, begin by drawing a door and windows. Using the X-acto knife cut out the door shape only on three sides, leaving a long edge for folding back so door will open and close.

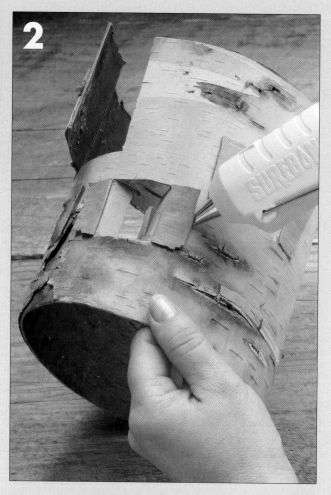

2 Cut windows first down the middle and on top, leaving sides to be folded back. From the inside of the bark, score areas to be folded. Fold back door and windows. The bark on the windows can be separated and folded to make shutters on the inside and outside. With glue gun, glue shutters to outside of house.

3 Measure the width of the top of the house. Collecting sticks together lay out enough sticks in length to cover top of house, add an extra 1 inch to each side. Cut a length of wire double the length of the row of sticks adding an extra 3 inches for twisting together. Wrap wire around the first stick $\frac{1}{2}$ inch from end, twist together with a small pliers. Add the next stick in the roll using the same method. Secure ends. Repeat by cutting another length of wire using this method for the other end of the sticks. You'll now have a bendable roof form. To make into a curved shape, add a curved support under the roll of bendable sticks.

4 Pinecones can be wired to the house, by cutting two small slits in the bark. Wrapping a wire length around the pinecones, insert wires into the slits and twist together on the inside, to secure pinecones in place. Using glue gun, place and glue reindeer moss and leaves to roof form.

5 Create a path leading up to the house with small stones or broken pieces of flagstone. Scatter reindeer moss near house and sprinkle with glitter. Add a mirror lake, a seashell bird-bath, pinecone bushes.

TAKE NOTE

Create your own fairies, making them out of nature's materials. Make a face and hat from acorns, a body from pinecones, twigs for arms and legs, and leaves for wings.

Decorative Bi-Level Birdhouse

This decorative cedar birdhouse will look nice on a porch or patio. It also becomes a conversation piece. Birds love it too!

BEFORE YOU BEGIN

The finished measurements are 10 inches wide by 15 inches high by $7\frac{1}{4}$ inches deep. It will take about two hours depending on abilities with a saw, drill and hammer. The dimensions were determined to best utilize the size of the lumber. The cost is around $7.00 and utilizes a 6-foot piece of 1 by 8 cedar lumber. Always use the rough side of cedar as the outside of project. This project would also look good using only the first level.

This birdhouse is made using basic cutting skills and a few simple 45-degree angles. The combination of rough cedar and twigs makes it blend well with nature and the outdoors. More twigs and even pinecones and moss could be added for more interest.

TOOLS NEEDED
- ❑ Nails—$1\frac{1}{2}$-inch finishing nails— about 35
- ❑ Wood glue
- ❑ Table or radial-arm saw
- ❑ Drill with small bit for starting nail holes, 1-inch Forstner or wood bore bit and a bit to fit twigs for perches
- ❑ Hammer

MATERIALS NEEDED
- ❑ 6-foot piece of 1 by 8 cedar rough-cut lumber (actually measures $\frac{3}{4}$ inch by about $7\frac{1}{4}$ inches)
- ❑ Twigs, short lengths of about $\frac{3}{8}$ inch in diameter and $\frac{3}{4}$ to 1 inch in diameter

HOW TO MAKE A DECORATIVE BI-LEVEL BIRDHOUSE

2 Drill four pilot holes in level one back piece, $\frac{3}{8}$ inch from edges at lower corners and about $1\frac{1}{2}$ inches below roof line. Line up sides, back and base with back facing up. Nail in place. As you work on the project, make sure the pieces line up flush with one another as shifting may occur while nailing. At bottom sides, $\frac{3}{8}$ inch from bottom edge and $1\frac{1}{2}$ inches from back edge, drill pilot holes for nails to hold base in place. Also drill two pilot holes $\frac{3}{8}$ inch from front side edges. Nail in place. For the front piece, repeat process as for the back piece.

1 Mark and cut the following pieces according to the layout: for the front and back of first level—$7\frac{1}{4}$ inches wide (width of board) with sides of 6 inches and about $4\frac{1}{2}$ inches—cut short side of roof at 45-degree angle, cutting through to opposite side of board (this will create the roof line of next piece to cut); for level one roof pieces, use the width of the board and cut one $7\frac{3}{4}$ inches long and one $5\frac{1}{2}$ inches long; for sides of level two, cut two pieces $3\frac{1}{4}$ inches wide and 3 inches long; for level two roof piece, cut 6 inches wide and 7 inches long; for the base, cut $4\frac{1}{2}$ inches wide and $5\frac{1}{2}$ inches long; for level one sides, cut one $4\frac{1}{2}$ inches wide and 6 inches long and one $4\frac{1}{2}$ inches wide and $4\frac{1}{4}$ inches long (measure short side of cut front piece, to verify this measurement, in case the angles were a bit off); for level two front and back pieces, find center measurement of board (it should be about $3\frac{5}{8}$ inches from both edges) and make a cut lengthwise at least 7 or 8 inches; cut the angled pieces from the two blocks of wood. Measure 4 inches on straight sides and cut the 45-degree angles as shown on layout. Label the pieces for ease of identification. Drill 1-inch holes in front of level one as indicated on the layout. Drill a 1-inch hole in a level two side piece as indicated. Drill holes about $\frac{3}{4}$ inch below the two bird holes on level one front piece for twig perches. Use bit size according to size of twigs.

3 Line up the longer level one roof piece with the top edge of roof line and with front and back edges extending $\frac{1}{2}$ inch. Drill pilot holes 1 inch in from front and back edges, $\frac{1}{4}$ inch from top and 2 inches in from bottom edges of roof pieces. Nail in place. Line up shorter level one roof piece with top edge of roof to create the point. Drill pilot holes 1 inch in from sides and $1\frac{1}{4}$ inches from top and bottom edges of roof. Nail in place.

4 For level two, line up front angle pieces with side piece with hole. The bottom of the side piece should be even with lower wide angle. Drill pilot holes in angled front piece, $3/8$ inch from side edge, $1\frac{1}{2}$ inches in from top point and 1 inch in from bottom edge. Nail in place. Tip: Place other side piece at other end to hold level while drilling and nailing. Place remaining side piece along other edge, lining up top edge of side piece with top wide angle of front angled piece. Drill pilot holes as for other side. Make sure pieces are flush and nail in place. Repeat the process for back piece. For level two roof, drill pilot holes 1 inch from front and back edges and $1\frac{1}{2}$ inches in from top and bottom of roof edge. Place roof on level two, with $3/4$ inch extending at top and bottom and $1/2$ inch in from front and back edges. Nail in place.

5 To secure level two to level one, drill pilot holes on the side without the hole, about 1 inch from bottom on side of front and back piece and at a slight downward angle. Nail in place. Use wood glue between level two and top of level one roof, to secure the side with the hole.

6 While glue is drying, cut two pieces of twigs, 3 inches long, for filling in spaces on level two at roof line with level one and roof line on level two above bird hole. Cut a larger twig about 4 inches long for below the level two side with hole. Cut two twigs $1\frac{1}{2}$ inches long, for perch on level one front. Glue twigs in place.

TEA PARTY

Enjoy some time sitting in your garden or gathering with friends and sharing a cup of tea.

BEFORE YOU BEGIN

Here our cup of tea holds more than a warm drink; we gather together the flowers, leaves, herbs and softness of light. Gather together all the elements that make a garden grow—light, water, earth. Add plants, watch it grow in light, smell and taste the sweetness of what a garden cup of tea can be!

You can purchase new teacups or teapots for this project or search for great finds at garage or estate sales where you can creatively mix and match various saucers and cups.

TOOLS NEEDED
❑ SEE THE DETAILED LIST WITH EACH OF THE PROJECTS.

MATERIALS NEEDED
❑ SEE THE DETAILED LIST WITH EACH OF THE PROJECTS.

HOW TO MAKE A TEA PARTY

MATERIALS NEEDED

❏ TEACUPS
❏ SMALL ROCKS
❏ POTTING SOIL
❏ SEEDS OR TRANSPLANTS
❏ DECORATIVE MOSS

FLORAL CUP

1 Begin by filling the teacup one-fourth full of small rocks to aid in soil drainage.

2 Fill cup up to within $\frac{1}{2}$ inch of the top with potting soil.

3 If planting seeds, follow packet instructions for depth and coverage of seeds. If planting a transplant, remove enough of the soil to make room for the roots of the transplant and cover again to $\frac{1}{2}$ inch of top of cup.

4 Cover top of teacup with decorative moss. Water daily, as the small surface area of the cup absorbs water quickly.

TEA LIGHT

1 Fill teacup to within 1 inch of top with fine sand.

2 Center a tea light candle in the middle of the cup and press into the sand.

3 Decorate outer edge of cup with leaves or flower petals to make a unique surface design.

MATERIALS NEEDED

❏ TEACUP
❏ FINE SAND
❏ TEA LIGHT CANDLE
❏ LEAVES OR FLOWER
  PETALS

TAKE NOTE

The many combinations of herbs and flowers create varied aromas and tastes, as well as medicinal treatments. For calming or relaxing try combinations of: lavender, lemon balm, sweet marjoram, chamomile, sage, thyme and rosemary. For stomach or headaches try: peppermint, chamomile, lavender and rosemary. For reducing a fever: basil, catmint, marigold flowers, sage, thyme and angelica. For coughs and colds: rose, fennel, sage, thyme and fennel.

The true tea plant, Camellia sinensis, can be grown and harvested for black or green tea leaves. Black tea leaves are hand rolled and allowed to oxidize for several hours before drying. Green tea can be used fresh or dried immediately. Camellia sinensis grows in Zones 6-9.

CUP OF TEA

1 Boil water and prewarm teapot or teacup. Use ½ teaspoon of dried herbs or flowers, 2 to 3 teaspoons of fresh herbs or flowers to each cup of water. Add boiling water, cover and steep for 10 minutes.

2 Strain tea by pouring it through a strainer. Small muslin bags are available to make your own teabags or a teaball can also be used in place of using a strainer.

3 Sun tea can also be made by leaving herbs and flowers in a covered glass jar in the hot sun for several hours. Strain tea into cups, sweeten with honey and refrigerate remaining tea.

MATERIALS NEEDED

❏ TEAPOT, OR TEACUP
❏ VARIETY OF GARDEN HERBS AND FLOWERS INCLUDING: CHAMOMILE, MARIGOLD, LAVENDER, JASMINE, LEMONGRASS, ROSEMARY, SAGE, THYME, SPEARMINT, PEPPERMINT, LEMON BALM, FENNEL, LEMON VERBENA, RASPBERRY LEAVES, SWEET MARJORAM, BASIL, CATMINT, ANGELICA, NASTURTIUM, SCENTED GERANIUM, ANISE, CHERVIL, TARRAGON, SUMMER SAVORY
❏ BOILING WATER
❏ HONEY

CHANGING GARDEN VIEW

Visualize new combinations of color, texture and design by creating a garden wheel. Picture a garden that can wonderfully change with a sleight of hand and no digging. Rotating the leaves of this garden wheel lets you see how to create harmonious garden combinations.

BEFORE YOU BEGIN

Explore changing color with a color wheel, putting monochromatic combinations of lights and darks of a single color together. This change in hues visually expands and defines each color you use. Look at an analogous color scheme of colors that are close to each other, like yellow and orange, to bring out the intensity of each other's color. Use complementary colors, warm and cool tones next to each other, to create drama and definition in a color scheme.

A wheel of garden textures will help to show the effect that shape and surface make in creating a textural tapestry in the garden. Juxtaposing linear foliage shapes with strong bold or light ferny shapes creates dimension that lasts all season long. A perennial-annual wheel creatively adds, subtracts or multiplies color, texture and design as each season changes the garden. Combine the tried and true of your perennial garden with what's new and exciting in each season's annuals.

1 Create the outline design, trace 12 times onto heavyweight paper, and cut out these 12 design pieces.

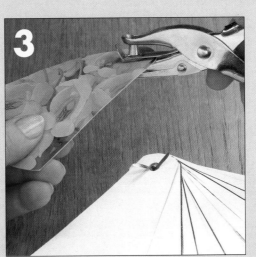

3 Punch outlines' holes with hole punch as shown. Gather all 12 pieces together using brad fastener to bind them.

4 Fan out to make a complete circle. Shift each piece to form a variety of visual combinations.

2 Pick your own garden photographs or find photos in magazines of plant images you would like on your garden wheel. Trace 12 photos with the outline design from step 1. Cut out and, using glue stick, glue the photos onto each of the cutout heavyweight papers. You'll now have 12 picture designs.

HARVEST WREATH

Collect remnants from your garden, or visit a market or garden center to acessorize this harvest wreath.

BEFORE YOU BEGIN

In fall the leaves of the boxwood become leathery and gleam a rich, dark green. Holly produces its crimson berries and winterberry glistens on bare branches. There may be a few fruits and vegetables left in the garden, but no matter if your garden is completely bereft. These materials are available at food markets and garden centers so you can construct a harvest wreath with materials you select in your shopping basket. Actual quantities of each doesn't matter. Think of this wreath as a big stew. Any fruit or vegetable that is small, colorful and firm will work in almost any proportion.

TOOLS NEEDED

- ❏ FLORIST'S WOOD PICKS WITHOUT WIRE OR STURDY TWIGS 4 FEET LONG, ONE FOR EACH FRUIT OR VEGETABLE
- ❏ FLORAL SHEARS

MATERIALS NEEDED

- ❏ ASSORTMENT OF FRUITS AND VEGGIES SUCH AS:
- ❏ 3 LARGE AND 6 SMALL ARTICHOKES
- ❏ 3 SMALL LEMONS, BRUSSELS SPROUTS, TURNIPS, SMALL APPLES, VERY FIRM HOT PEPPERS
- ❏ 5 TO 6 STEMS WINTER BERRY, FIRETHORN OR HOLLY BERRY, SIX TO EIGHT INCHES LONG
- ❏ 4 TO 6 STEMS HOLLY LEAVES OR OREGON GRAPE HOLLY, SIX TO EIGHT INCHES LONG
- ❏ FRESH BOXWOOD WREATH PURCHASED FROM A GARDEN CENTER

HOW TO MAKE A HARVEST WREATH

HANDY HINTS

To Buy or Not To Buy. If you buy the boxwood wreath base, decorating is a snap. Or make your own base by wrapping eight-inch sprigs of boxwood around a sturdy wreath frame with florist spool wire.

1 Each pick must have a point at both ends. Florist's picks typically have a point at only one end. Take the shears and with one snip, cut a point at the opposite end. If you're using twigs, you'll have to cut points at both ends. Insert a pick into the base of each fruit or vegetable. The moisture in the fruit will cause the pick to swell slightly, ensuring a firm attachment. Cut the picks shorter if necessary for the small items.

2 Ready-made wreaths are constructed with wire wrapping. Place the largest elements on the wreath first by slipping a pick under the wrapping, dividing the wreath in thirds; at 12 o'clock, 4 o'clock and 8 o'clock. Start with the three big artichokes. Then put a lemon in position between each artichoke, always slipping the pick under a wire to hold it.

3 Keep adding materials, going in order of size. Here the turnips and apples would be next; then small artichokes, peppers and Brussels sprouts. When you get to the smallest items, they can be inserted at random, wherever you find a space.

4 Tuck in the sprigs of berries and the extra pieces of holly foliage anywhere it looks a little sparse.

TAKE NOTE

Whether hung outdoors or inside, the cooler the temperature, the longer this wreath will last. Keep out of direct sunlight. In very cold weather outdoors, it can withstand a drop to below freezing without any damage and will last 3 to 4 weeks.

If hung on a door, its best placed where the door isn't in constant use with crowds of people brushing by.

This wreath is also perfect for a centerpiece on the dining room table or on a buffet. Just make sure if you are laying it flat that you have decorated the inside of the ring and the outside as well, and not simply the top surface.

CLAY POT WIND CHIMES

This wind chime looks and sounds beautiful — naturally!

TOOLS NEEDED

❏ DRILL
❏ ¼-INCH DRILL BIT
❏ ¼-INCH GLASS/TILE BIT
❏ PINCH CLOTHESPINS

BEFORE YOU BEGIN

Use a variety of sizes of small clay pots and a birch branch, to make this natural looking wind chime for the porch, patio or garden. Embellish it with rusted tin or copper shapes that you can make or purchase at the craft store. For added interest the rims of the pots can be painted, sponged or stenciled with garden-related designs. This project will take about an hour and costs about $9.00 depending on the cost of embellishments.

MATERIALS NEEDED

❏ 5 CLAY POTS IN VARYING
   SIZES (1½-, 3- OR 4-
   INCH) PLUS BROKEN CLAY
   PIECES
❏ JUTE—3-PLY OR ANY
   APPROPRIATE ROPE
❏ BIRCH BRANCH ABOUT 2
   INCHES IN DIAMETER
   AND 18 TO 20 INCHES
   LONG
❏ RUSTED TIN SHAPES OR
   CUT COPPER SHAPES

1 Cut birch branch to 18 or 20 inches. Line up the five clay pots next to birch branch, spacing them about 1 inch apart. Decide on the most attractive way for the branch to hang. Mark placement of center of each pot on birch branch. Then mark two holes, about ¾ inch from each end of branch, for rope for hanging. Drill holes.

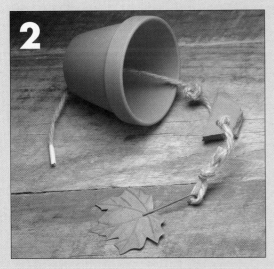

2 Choose five pieces of broken clay pot that will fit as the clapper for each pot. Using the glass/tile drill bit, drill holes in each broken piece. To prepare the clay pots for hanging, cut five pieces of jute about 24 inches long. Tie a loop knot at one end and about 2 inches from that knot, tie another knot. String the appropriate broken clay piece on to the jute.

3 Cut about 64 inches of jute. Double the jute and string through the outside holes, leaving the ends at the bottom side of branch. Tie them in a few knots, large enough not to go through the holes. String the five clay pots through the appropriate holes, in descending size. Place pinch clothespins to hold each one in place. Hang project from something like a doorknob and adjust the length of jute to make clay pots line up. When satisfied with placement tie knots at top of each one, large enough not to go through the holes. Clip extra jute above knot to about ½ inch.

HANDY HINTS

To make the jute go through the small hole of the clay pots, wrap a small piece of masking tape around tip of jute. When jute is through clay pot hole, hold it up to decide on the placement of the knot that will hold pot in place. Mark, remove from pot and tie two to three knots that will be large enough to hold the pot in place. Put pot back on jute. Hang decorative tin or copper shape on loop at end and secure in place.

TWIG GARDEN SIGN

Make a natural and unique garden sign from twigs. It is easy and will add to your garden, whether it is hung from the garden fence or staked into the ground.

BEFORE YOU BEGIN

This project can be made any size; however the diameter of the twigs will determine the size of the sign. The project shown here is 7$\frac{1}{4}$ inches by 24 inches. Look for very straight twigs, like willow. It is fine if there are knots, branch nodules or a slightly curved area. When using any natural element, use irregularities to an advantage. Natural elements will not be even or line up perfectly, which is the beauty of them. This all adds to the unique appeal of projects from natural elements.

The garden sign will take about 1$\frac{1}{2}$ hours depending on abilities with a saw, drill and hammer. The cost is minimal as the willow twigs can be found in nature. The only cost is about $6.00 for the cedar board.

2 Cut with miter saw. Be sure to cut small pieces and angles at end of twig first to have something to hold on to as cutting. Arrange cut pieces on cedar board as shown in layout. Create a baseline with masking tape or a yardstick about 1$\frac{1}{2}$ inches from bottom edge of board. Place the letters about $\frac{1}{2}$ to $\frac{3}{4}$ inch apart. Some letters may go a bit higher or lower depending on knots or other irregularities. Use these irregularities to an advantage to give the sign character. When satisfied with the arrangement begin to nail the pieces to the board by drilling pilot holes into twigs. Do one twig at a time and one letter at a time. Two holes are needed for the long pieces, and one for shorter pieces.

1 Cut 48-inch cedar board in half. One half will be for sign and the other for the stakes. Measure and mark with masking tape the following lengths of twigs: two at 4$\frac{1}{2}$ inches; eight at 4 inches; one at 3 inches; two at 2$\frac{1}{2}$ inches; one at 2$\frac{1}{4}$ inches; three at 2 inches; two at 1$\frac{3}{4}$ inches; two at 1$\frac{1}{2}$ inches; one at 1 inch; one at $\frac{3}{4}$ inch. Place smaller pieces and one with angles at one end of twig for easier cutting. Label each piece with masking tape, by the letter it belongs to. Referring to layout, mark pieces to be cut at an angle. All angles are about 45 degrees except for the 1-inch piece cut at a slight angle for the "A".

3 Stakes can be cut from remaining cedar board. Cut stakes about 2 inches wide and use the full length on board. Cut one end of each stake to a point. Use two wood screws at top of each stake on back side of sign to hold stakes in place. Sign may also be hung. Use two medium-sized eyelet screws at top of sign and use small rope to hang sign.

KITCHEN

*F*or someone who loves crafting, the kitchen presents an interesting blend. Of course, a person spends a lot of time in the kitchen, and you want it to look nice. But the kitchen is also a place for creating delicious food— maybe even from the bounty of your own garden! From decorative serving ideas and attractive wreaths (on the decorating side) to a bowl of frosted fruit or a strawberry and herb tree (on the edible side), these ideas and instructions will make your kitchen a lovely place to be ... and a forum for some culinary adventure too.

CARVED WATERMELON CENTERPIECE

Remember eating watermelon at summer picnics and barbecues as a child? This craft uses that favorite summertime food and takes it beyond taste alone, to include stunning visual appeal.

BEFORE YOU BEGIN

We all anticipate the fall season and the fun that it brings with carving pumpkins to adorn our doorsteps and tables. This great craft is not limited to the short season of fall because it uses the bounty of summer year-round by creating a carved centerpiece using a watermelon instead of a pumpkin. A watermelon is expertly carved using a relief-style carving technique to create a stunning design on the skin of the watermelon. This technique is easy to learn and when the project is complete it will leave the sculptor feeling like an artist. Unlike a carved pumpkin, the watermelon can be eaten when the centerpiece is no longer needed, making it a truly edible and multifunctional centerpiece!

The watermelon is carved to become a centerpiece for a buffet or picnic table and also functions as a serving bowl to hold a rainbow of summer fruits, a recipe of homemade fruit punch or even a bouquet of edible flowers from the garden.

TOOLS NEEDED
- ❏ ¼-INCH WOOD CHISEL
- ❏ X-ACTO KNIFE
- ❏ MASKING TAPE
- ❏ SPOON
- ❏ PARING KNIFE

MATERIALS NEEDED
- ❏ WATERMELON
- ❏ ASSORTED FRUITS
- ❏ GRAPE LEAVES

HOW TO MAKE A CARVED WATERMELON CENTERPIECE

1 Wipe the surface of the watermelon with paper towels until completely dry to avoid having any moisture on its surface; this will help the tape stick to the watermelon's skin and hold the grape leaves securely in place for carving. Using the masking tape, creatively arrange and tape the grape leaves to the surface of the skin of the watermelon.

TAKE NOTE

When choosing a watermelon to carve, pick one that is dark green in color and has very few blemishes or bumps on the watermelon's skin surface. This will make the design easier to carve and the finished watermelon centerpiece will look its best.

HANDY HINTS

If while the centerpiece is on display the carved surface of the watermelon becomes dry looking and the design starts to shrivel, spray the carved portion lightly with butter-flavored cooking spray to help moisten it.

2 Be sure to tape the leaves securely to the surface of the watermelon; this will make it easier to carve the impression of them onto the skin of the melon.

TAKE NOTE

If grape leaves are hard to find, use leaves such as oak or maple that can be found in your backyard in place of them or create your own design such as carving monogram initials or words onto the watermelon.

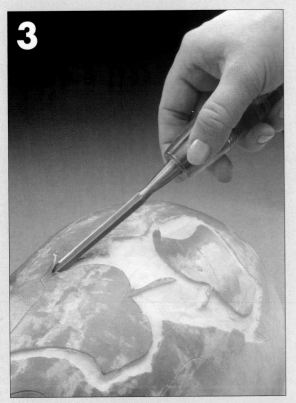

3 Using the tip of an X-acto knife, carefully cut around the outside edges of the secured leaves. This step is simply tracing the design of the grape leaves using an X-acto knife in place of a pencil or pen. Cut the lines about an eighth of an inch deep. This will be deep enough to penetrate the skin, but not so deep that the knife cuts into the flesh of the watermelon. When finished carving, remove the tape and the grape leaves from the watermelon's surface and discard them. You will clearly see the outline of the grape leaves made by cutting with the X-acto knife.

4 Using the tip of the X-acto knife, cut a scalloped or zigzagged shaped border around the grape leaf impressions to frame them in. Using the wood chisel, gently carve away all of the unwanted skin of the watermelon to expose the design of the grape leaves. While you carve, be sure to carve lightly enough so that the fleshy portion of the watermelon underneath the skin is not gouged. Only a small amount of pressure applied to the wood chisel is needed to remove the skin and expose the design of the leaves. Gouging the flesh of the watermelon will take away from the beauty of the finished centerpiece.

5 Remove the top of the watermelon using a paring knife by making zigzagged shaped cuts around the top surface of the watermelon. Make two to three more cuts across the surface of the top to remove it in pieces. Carefully and gently remove the top of the melon by prying it off using the tip of the paring knife or a spoon.

6 Remove the flesh of the watermelon with a spoon to create a bowl to be filled with fruit, fruit punch or a bouquet of edible flowers. The flesh of the melon can be cut and then mixed with other fruits such as honeydew melon, strawberries, blackberries, raspberries, kiwi, starfruit, apples or oranges to create a stunning fruit bowl.

7 The fruit bowl can be made up to two days in advance by spraying the carved surface with water, covering it with wet paper towels and covering tightly with plastic wrap. The centerpiece should not be filled with fruit, fruit punch or edible flowers until on display.

DRIED APPLE DECORATOR WREATH

This multipurpose wreath, crafted from dehydrated apples that have been sprinkled with cinnamon and a slight hint of nutmeg, is as fragrant as it is beautiful.

BEFORE YOU BEGIN

Who ever said not to play with your food? This great craft, the Dried Apple Decorator Wreath, lets us do just that by creating a work of art from apples. There are many methods to dehydrate fruit; but this technique is very easy and the end result will leave you feeling completely satisfied. In this project a simple straw wreath is embellished with cinnamon-and-nutmeg-scented dehydrated apples from the fall harvest, and a silk ribbon adds the crowning touch to quickly make this craft become your favorite and leave any room smelling like a freshly baked apple pie.

Apples from the fall harvest are hot-glued to a straw wreath to create a stunning work of art to hang on any wall or become an elegant charger plate to hold a piece of fine china for your next dinner party.

TOOLS NEEDED

❑ CHEF'S KNIFE
❑ CLEAN METAL SCREEN OR WIRE BAKING RACKS
❑ HOT GLUE GUN WITH GLUE STICKS

MATERIALS NEEDED

❑ APPLES
❑ ¼ CUP CINNAMON
❑ 1 TABLESPOON NUTMEG
❑ 1 CUP LEMON JUICE
❑ SPRAY VARNISH
❑ EUCALYPTUS WREATH OR OTHER WREATH CREATED FROM GREENERY
❑ 2 YARDS SILK WIRED RIBBON
❑ FLORIST WIRE
❑ WIRE HANGER, IF DESIRED

HOW TO MAKE A DRIED APPLE DECORATOR WREATH

HANDY HINTS

Personalize the wreaths by adding different embellishments such as gilded lemon leaves, pinecones, bows, miniature flags, flowers or anything that would personalize the wreath.

1 Heat oven to 195°F. Stir together ¼ cup cinnamon and 1 tablespoon nutmeg in a small bowl. Using a chef's knife, slice the apples into quarter-inch-thick slices horizontally to expose the apple's star shape in the center. Place lemon juice in medium-sized bowl and dip the apples in the lemon juice to prevent them from turning brown.

HANDY HINTS

The apples can also be dehydrated using a commercial dehydrator; just follow the manufacturer's instruction manual for specific details on how to dehydrate apples.

2 Sprinkle the slices with the cinnamon and nutmeg mixture. A powdered sugar shaker that can be purchased at a cooking supply store works well for sprinkling or dusting the mixture with less mess. Place the apple slices onto a piece of clean metal screen or wire baking racks. Bake 4 hours. Turn the oven off and leave the apples in the oven with the door closed for at least 8 hours or overnight. Do not open the oven door because all of the remaining heat is needed to slowly dehydrate the apple slices. If using a wire screen, wash it in hot soapy water, dry it as usual, roll it up and tie with string to store it for another use.

3 Spray both sides of the apple slices with spray varnish, following the manufacturer's instructions. Using the hot glue gun, individually glue the apple slices to the straw wreath, overlapping as needed. Fill in spaces that are empty with more of the apple slices or place an additional layer of apples on top of the original layer to achieve the desired fullness of the wreath.

HANDY HINTS

Most of the items such as spray varnish, wreath, ribbon, florist's wire, wire hanger and glue gun can be purchased at any craft store. The wire screen can be purchased at a hardware store.

4 Make a bow using the silk ribbon and attach it at the top of the wreath using florist's wire to hold the bow in place at the center. Fasten the wire hanger to the back of the wreath if needed or use the wreath as a charger plate liner for dinnerware.

HANDY HINTS

Dried leaves can often become very brittle and break. To help preserve them, mix one part glycerin to one part very hot tap water and brush or spray this solution onto the leaves to make them soft and flexible. Let them dry completely before attaching the apples. Glycerin is a product that is used to soften dry hands and can be purchased over the counter at most pharmacies.

TAKE NOTE

When creating the apple wreath, you may choose any color apples you have on hand or mix and match colors for different and unique results. Ripe but firm apples with no blemishes or bruises will work best for this craft.

INFUSED VINEGARS

Making infused vinegars is a great way to bottle the essence of the summer's harvest.

TOOL NEEDED
❏ BAKING SHEET

MATERIALS NEEDED
❏ INGREDIENTS FOR RECIPES
❏ DECORATIVE GLASS JARS, BOTTLES OR DECANTERS

BEFORE YOU BEGIN

Infused vinegars are a great way to capture summer in no time at all. Included are recipes for making pepper-infused or minted berry-infused vinegars. Experiment on your own with various combinations of herbs, berries and seasoning depending on what is in season to create your own flavors. Freezing, canning and drying the harvest require time and if time is an issue, this is the project for you! With no special equipment or processing required, these infused vinegars will add summertime flavor to all of your year-round cooking. Infused vinegars can make great gifts or decorations for the kitchen when stored in decorative glass containers.

Smoky Roasted Red Pepper Vinegar

2 red bell peppers
1 tablespoon vegetable oil
1 tablespoon chipotle pepper in adobo sauce
1 cup white wine vinegar

Smoky Roasted Red Pepper Vinegar

Preheat oven to 450°F. Rub the bell peppers with vegetable oil and place on baking sheet. Bake until skin of peppers is charred and blackened, about 20 to 30 minutes. Remove peppers and place in a resealable plastic bag until skin softens, about 10 to 15 minutes. Peel the charred skin under running water. Cut peppers in half and remove seeds and membranes. Puree bell peppers and chipotle pepper in a blender until smooth and creamy, add vinegar and blend until just combined. Place in a sterilized glass jar in the refrigerator until vinegar is full flavored, about 10 to 14 days. Store, covered, in the refrigerator.

TAKE NOTE

Use infused flavored vinegars in all your favorite recipes such as salad dressing or sauces or add them to preserves or jams to make a glaze for grilling meats or baking roasts.

Gently heat vinegar in a saucepan until just warm; boiling the vinegar will destroy the natural properties. Warming it speeds up the release of flavors.

Infused vinegars make lovely kitchen decorations or gifts for giving. Pick out interesting shapes and decorations on bottles or use decorative decanters to store them in.

Any type of vinegar can be used for infusing vinegars, but a clear vinegar such as white wine vinegar will allow you to see the herbs, berries and seasonings.

Infused vinegars will normally keep for up to six months; store as indicated on recipe.

Minted Berry Vinegar

2 cups blueberries
1 cup lightly packed mint sprigs
1½ cups white wine vinegar

Sterilize a 4-cup glass jar. Place blueberries and mint in jar. Heat vinegar in small saucepan over medium heat until vinegar is warm but not hot. Pour vinegar over blueberries and mint.

Cover and let stand at room temperature 7 to 14 days or until vinegar is full flavored. Strain vinegar; place in sterilized bottle. Add fresh whole blueberries and mint leaves for garnish, if desired. Store at room temperature.

Minted Berry Vinegar

SQUASH VASE WITH FRUIT AND VEGETABLE FLOWERS

This vase is a fragrant and edible centerpiece created from the bounty of the garden; made by carving a simple but elegant design onto the skin of a squash and filling it with a bouquet of flowers made from fruits and vegetables.

BEFORE YOU BEGIN

Not only do we relish the taste of the garden, but also its visual appeal. This elaborate table decoration, made from the garden's bounty, is sure to delight and please all the dinner guests at your party. The fun centerpiece boasts edible vegetable flowers that are simple enough for even children to create and will have them wanting to eat their veggies! The flowers are placed on wooden skewers and then arranged into a carved squash to create a homemade centerpiece to adorn your table. Since food is a joy for all the senses, this great craft truly has it all. Be sure to remove the skewers if your guests are planning on eating your craft or make extra edible flowers without the skewers and arrange them on a platter with dip for your guests to enjoy.

TOOLS NEEDED
- ❏ CHEF'S KNIFE
- ❏ PARING KNIFE
- ❏ VARIOUS FLOWER- OR STAR-SHAPED COOKIE CUTTERS
- ❏ MELON BALLER OR SMALL SPOON
- ❏ CUTTING BOARD

MATERIALS NEEDED
- ❏ WOODEN SKEWERS OF VARIOUS LENGTHS
- ❏ SQUASH WITH A FAIRLY SOFT SHELL SUCH AS SPAGHETTI OR BUTTERNUT
- ❏ COLORED BELL PEPPERS
- ❏ GREEN ONIONS
- ❏ BLACKBERRIES, BLUE-BERRIES OR RASPBERRIES
- ❏ LARGE BOWL OF ICE WATER

HOW TO MAKE A SQUASH VASE WITH FRUIT AND VEGETABLE FLOWERS

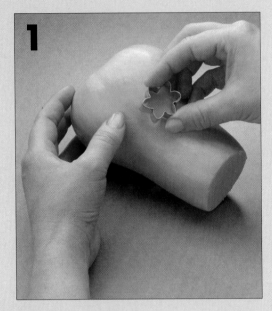

Squash Vase

1 Place the squash onto a cutting board. Using a chef's knife, cut off a small portion of the bottom of the squash to be sure the base is even and will not tip over while standing.

Slice off one to two inches of the stem end of the squash to create a place to insert the flower skewers.

Using a melon baller, small star- or flower-shaped cookie cutter, firmly press the cutter or melon baller into the squash shell about one-eighth to one-quarter inch deep.

2 Remove the cutter or melon baller and using a small spoon, gently remove the impressed design with the tip of the spoon. Make several impressions with the melon baller or cookie cutter in different places on the skin of the squash to create a design.

The squash vase can be made one to two days ahead by storing it in the refrigerator covered with damp paper towels and plastic wrap. Arrange the flowers into the squash vase and place on a decorative plate or platter to display. Be sure to remove the skewers from the flowers if you plan on eating them.

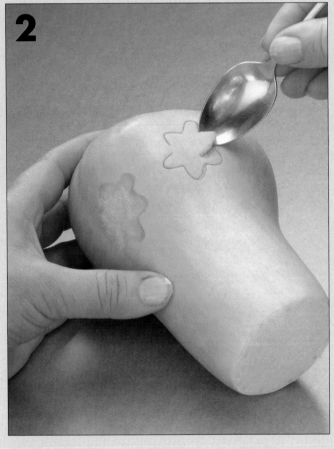

OOPS!

If the flowers slip down the skewers, cut a small baby carrot in half, place it on the wooden skewer and slip the flower over the top of it. The carrot will become an anchor for the flower.

Colored Bell Pepper Flowers

3 Using a chef's knife, slice off one quarter to one third of the pepper and remove the stem and seeds.

Lay the cut portion of the pepper onto a cutting board with the inner flesh of the pepper facing up.

Using a flower- or star-shaped cookie cutter, cut the shape from the pepper slice. Gently remove the flower from the cutter and place it onto the end of a wooden skewer.

Top the flower with a blackberry, raspberry or blueberry. Repeat with remaining peppers. The flowers can be made up to one day ahead by storing them in the refrigerator covered with damp paper towels and plastic wrap. Arrange the flowers into the squash vase.

Green Onion Flowers

4 Lay the onion down onto a cutting board and using a paring knife, cut off the root end, making sure to remove the entire root. If any of the root is left, it will hinder the onion flower from opening up completely.

Cut off and remove the dark green portion of the onion so that the remainder of the onion is four to five inches long.

Make six to eight one-inch vertical cuts at the bulb end of the onion. Rotate the onion 90 degrees and repeat cuts.

Place the flower in the ice water until the flower blooms and opens up. Repeat with remaining onions. The temperature of the water will determine how fast the flower will open up; colder water will speed up the process.

The flowers can be made and kept in the ice water in the refrigerator for up to two days. Slip the onion flowers onto the wooden skewers and arrange the skewers into the squash vase.

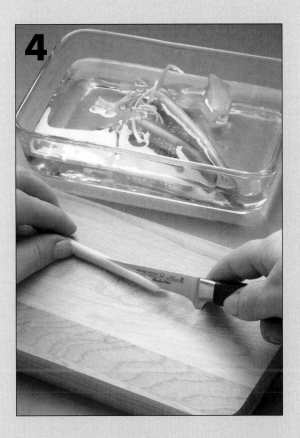

FROSTED FRUIT AND EDIBLE FLOWER BOWL

This versatile centerpiece is made using fresh fruit in season. Mix and match with whatever fruit you have on hand from your garden's bounty.

BEFORE YOU BEGIN

Add fresh herbs and edible flowers to the Frosted Fruit Bowl to give it natural garden beauty. "Frosting" the fruit is simple and will make the centerpiece elegant enough to serve at even the fanciest dinner parties or get-togethers.

The frosted fruits in this centerpiece mimic the look of a fresh winter frost when it coats the trees and bushes in a beautiful layer that glistens in the sun. As beautiful as this centerpiece is, it will take no time at all to create. "Frosting" fruit is easy and takes little time and effort. If you are looking to create a centerpiece that looks like you spent hours creating it but actually didn't, this is the centerpiece to make. Use whatever fruit you have on hand from the garden's bounty to create it or mix and match fruits according to the season. For example, use pears, golden apples and cranberries for a beautiful fall arrangement or citrus fruits, star fruits and mango for a summer Hawaiian-luau-themed centerpiece. Simply add greenery such as bay leaves, lemon leaves or any variety of fresh herbs to complete your look.

TOOLS NEEDED

❑ SMALL, NEW PAINTBRUSH
❑ WIRE WHISK
❑ BAKING SHEET

MATERIALS NEEDED

❑ EGG WHITES OR POWDERED EGG WHITES
❑ COARSE SUGAR CRYSTALS OR DECORATING SUGAR
❑ ASSORTED FRUIT IN SEASON
❑ WAX PAPER
❑ FRESH HERBS IN SEASON, SUCH AS ROSEMARY, MINT OR LEMON LEAVES
❑ EDIBLE FLOWERS
❑ DECORATIVE BOWLS, PLATTERS OR PLATES

TAKE NOTE

Powdered egg whites can be purchased at specialty cake decorating stores or through specialty catalogs.

1. Line the baking sheet with wax paper. In a large bowl, beat the egg whites until frothy. Using the paintbrush, brush the top half of each piece of fruit with a thin layer of the beaten egg whites, then sprinkle them with the sugar. Let stand until they are completely dry, about 30 minutes. If using powdered egg whites, mix three parts water to one part powdered egg whites in a large bowl and whisk until thoroughly mixed.

2. Lightly brush the powdered egg mixture onto the top half of each piece of fruit and then sprinkle with sugar. To frost the leaves, herbs and edible flowers, brush with egg and then sprinkle with sugar. Place the leaves onto the baking sheet until dry, about 15 minutes. Repeat with the edible flowers. Decoratively arrange the fruit, herbs and flowers into a bowl or onto a plate or platter. If using raw egg whites, be sure to wash the fruit thoroughly because raw egg white should not be eaten.

HANDY HINTS

Instead of using regular sugar, try using colored sugars to match the theme of your party. For example use red, white and blue colored sugars to give the frosted fruit, flowers and herbs a patriotic theme. Colored sugars can be purchased at specialty cake decorating stores or through specialty catalogs.

SALSAS

The word salsa brings classic home-style Mexican cooking immediately to mind. Not only is salsa a tried-and-true family favorite, but it also sings with freshness and is a satisfying traditional condiment. Salsa makes a great gift!

BEFORE YOU BEGIN

Salsas are a great way to use the bounty of the summer garden. Normally, what immediately comes to mind when we think of salsas is tomatoes, but don't put any limits on salsa! It can also be made using green tomatoes, pineapple or just about any fruit you can think of. Salsas can also be made using canned tomatoes, fruits or preserves. The endless possibilities are mind-boggling. Your imagination is the only limit when creating salsas. Included are recipes utilizing tomatoes, pineapple and even mango.

Classic Tomato Salsa

Classic Tomato Salsa

5 Italian plum tomatoes, peeled, seeded and pureed
5 tablespoons tomato paste
10 tomatoes, peeled, seeded and chopped
½ cup chopped red onion
½ cup chopped Italian parsley
¼ cup chopped cilantro
1 jalapeño, seeded, minced
1 tablespoon white wine vinegar
1 tablespoon fresh oregano
1 teaspoon sugar
1 teaspoon garlic salt
½ teaspoon salt

In large mixing bowl, stir together the pureed tomatoes and tomato paste. Add remaining ingredients and stir to combine. Store in refrigerator.

Tropical Gingered Salsa

2 cups finely diced pineapple
½ cup finely diced mango
½ cup finely diced papaya
⅓ cup chopped cilantro
½ tablespoon finely chopped crystallized ginger
2 teaspoons lemon juice

In medium-sized bowl, stir together all ingredients. Store in refrigerator.

Speedy Traditional Pineapple Salsa

Speedy Traditional Pineapple Salsa

8-ounce can crushed pineapple
¼ cup orange marmalade
1 tablespoon orange zest
1 tablespoon chopped cilantro
1 tablespoon lime juice
1 jalapeño pepper, seeded and minced
¼ teaspoon salt

Place all ingredients in medium mixing bowl; stir to combine. Store in refrigerator.

TOOLS NEEDED

❑ MIXING BOWLS
❑ PARING KNIFE
❑ SPOON
❑ CHEF'S KNIFE

MATERIALS NEEDED

❑ INGREDIENTS FOR RECIPES

TAKE NOTE

Be creative when serving salsas. Serve them with tortilla chips, baked pita chips, bagel chips, crackers or even toasted slices of French bread, or serve them as a condiment for meats or fish or on a baked potato.

Homemade fresh salsas make great gifts. Package them in fun, decorative jars and containers. Make gift-giving baskets that include a jar of salsa with colored tortilla chips and place them in wicker baskets or decorative bags.

When making tomato salsas, fresh, ripe tomatoes usually work the best. If fresh tomatoes are not available, substitute a drained 28-ounce can of plum tomatoes for approximately $1\frac{1}{3}$ pounds of fresh tomatoes.

To peel tomatoes, cut an X at the bottom of the tomato and place them in simmering water until the skin is soft enough to peel away from the flesh.

PRESERVING THE HARVEST

Preserving fresh garden produce is a highly satisfying and surprisingly easy experience. It is a joy to preserve the fruit of your harvest, whether it is with a well-made jam or fruit spread, or even glazed onions. These items are not only wonderful to behold, but also a delight to eat.

BEFORE YOU BEGIN

There are different ways to preserve the harvest, but the end result is as satisfying to the soul as it is to the palate. Uncooked preserves, or freezer preserves, should be made using thoroughly ripe fruit, either fresh or frozen. Because the fruit is uncooked it retains maximum fruity and fresh taste compared to those that are canned and cooked. They are easy to fix and should always be stored in the freezer and they usually require more sugar than their cooked counterparts. The fruit spread included in this recipe can be made on the stove and kept in the refrigerator and the recipes require no special canning equipment. Onions are glazed with balsamic vinegar to make a great condiment for a steak or burger.

TOOL NEEDED
❏ POTATO MASHER

MATERIALS NEEDED
❏ LABELS
❏ JARS
❏ INGREDIENTS FOR RECIPES

Triple Berry Citrus Freezer Jam

Triple Berry Citrus Freezer Jam

2 cups crushed strawberries
½ cup raspberries, firmly packed
½ cup golden raspberries, firmly packed
3 tablespoons lemon juice
1 tablespoon lemon zest
1 tablespoon orange zest
1 package powdered pectin
½ cup dark corn syrup
3½ cups sugar

In large bowl, combine all berries, lemon juice, lemon zest and orange zest; stir well until combined. Slowly add pectin to the berry mixture, stirring constantly for two to three minutes. Slowly pour in corn syrup; stir well. Add sugar in a slow, steady stream, stirring well until sugar is dissolved. Ladle jam into freezer jars, leaving one-quarter inch of head space. Cover with two-piece lids. Let jam stand at room temperature until set, up to twenty-four hours, and then freeze.

Yield 3 pints

TAKE NOTE

Quantities can sometimes vary in recipes from what is stated on the recipe. It is difficult to tell because it will vary with the ripeness and juiciness of the fruit used or the thickness you prefer for your jam or fruit preserves.

TAKE NOTE

Before putting the fruit spread in the refrigerator, during the cooling process, cover the jars with a clean, dry kitchen towel to help the lids to seal.

Blackberry Orange Fruit Spread

3 cups blackberries
3 cups sugar
1 tablespoon grated orange peel
2 tablespoons orange juice

Combine all ingredients in a large saucepan. Gently mash the fruit using a potato masher and mash until well blended. Cook the fruit mixture over medium-high heat until mixture comes to a full boil, about 7 to 8 minutes. Boil the mixture, stirring continuously until the fruit spread has thickened. Ladle the warm fruit spread into clean, sterilized jars with sterilized two-piece lids. Seal lids and cool to room temperature. Store in the refrigerator.

Yield 3 cups

Blackberry Orange Fruit Spread

Balsamic and Thyme Glazed Baby Onions

¼ cup butter
2 pounds fresh small whole onions
1 cup balsamic vinegar
¼ cup brown sugar
2 teaspoons thyme, chopped
¾ teaspoon salt
¾ teaspoon freshly ground black pepper

Heat large nonstick sauté pan over medium heat. Add butter and stir until melted. Add onions and cook covered until onions are tender, about 15 to 20 minutes. Uncover and stir balsamic vinegar, brown sugar, thyme, salt and pepper into onions. Cook over medium heat, stirring frequently, until sugar has dissolved. Reduce heat to medium-low and continue to cook, stirring occasionally until liquid is thickened into a glaze, about 10 to 15 minutes. Store covered in the refrigerator for up to one week. Re-warm onions over medium-low heat before serving.

DOUBLE CHOCOLATE-DIPPED STRAWBERRY AND HERB TREE

This craft does double duty; it is a gorgeous centerpiece to grace your kitchen table or buffet, and can also be eaten as dessert!

BEFORE YOU BEGIN

This craft has endless possibilities. Its beauty can stand on its own as a centerpiece for a dessert buffet, grace the table at a Christmas party or bring it on a picnic for a dessert that is sure to be a hit. Double chocolate-dipped strawberries are secured to a floral pyramid-shaped foam block with toothpicks, and fresh rosemary sprigs or bay leaves are intermingled between them to add color as well as fragrance.

Add fresh blueberries to the Double Chocolate-Dipped Strawberry and Herb Tree and it will make a great Fourth of July decoration that will be patriotic with its red white and blue colors as well as a dessert that is as much fun as the fireworks. There is nothing better than fresh berries in the summer dipped in chocolate and when fresh rosemary or bay leaves are added, its fragrant smell will make any room smell as good as it looks.

TOOLS NEEDED
❏ BAKING SHEETS
❏ FORK OR SMALL SQUEEZE BOTTLE

MATERIALS NEEDED
❏ WAX PAPER
❏ FRESH STRAWBERRIES
❏ WHITE CHOCOLATE
❏ SEMISWEET CHOCOLATE
❏ ROUND TOOTHPICKS
❏ FRESH ROSEMARY OR BAY LEAVES
❏ GREEN FLORAL FOAM IN PYRAMID SHAPE, 12 BY 4 INCHES

HOW TO MAKE A DOUBLE CHOCOLATE-DIPPED STRAWBERRY AND HERB TREE

1 Rinse the strawberries under cool water and gently pat them dry with paper towels to remove any excess moisture. If the strawberries are not completely dry, the chocolate will not adhere as well. Line baking sheets with wax paper.

2 Place the white chocolate into a medium-sized microwave-able glass bowl. Microwave the chocolate on medium power for one minute and stir. Continue microwaving the chocolate in one-minute intervals until it is almost melted; stir the chocolate until smooth.

4 Place the semisweet chocolate into a medium-sized microwaveable glass bowl. Microwave the chocolate on medium power for one minute; stir. Continue microwaving the chocolate in one-minute intervals until it is almost melted, about two to three minutes longer; stir the chocolate until smooth. Using the tines of a fork or a small squeeze bottle, drizzle the melted dark chocolate over the white chocolate-dipped strawberries on the baking sheet.

3 Push each strawberry, stem end, onto the end of a tooth-pick. Dip each berry three fourths of the way into the melt-ed white chocolate, leaving the top of the berry and leaves uncoated. This will leave some of the pretty red color of the berries exposed. Place the chocolate-dipped berries onto the baking sheets lined with wax paper.

TAKE NOTE

Do not rinse the strawber-ries until just before you are ready to use them. Rinsing them ahead of time will cause them to become mushy and cause some of the color of the berries to bleed out.

5 Refrigerate the berries at least 20 to 30 minutes or until the chocolate is completely set and firm. When chocolate is set, push the toothpicks into the foam pyramid, starting at the top. If using fresh bay leaves, spear the bay leaves onto the opposite end of the toothpick before putting them onto the foam pyramid. If using fresh rosemary, push the stem end of the rosemary into the foam pyramid dispersed between the berries as desired. Using more rosemary will give the tree a fuller and greener look. Continue placing berries onto the foam pyramid starting at the top and working your way down to the bottom in a spiral fashion until the entire tree is covered.

HANDY HINTS

This centerpiece should be made and served on the same day. The berries will bleed or lose some of their moisture after they have been dipped, causing the chocolate to become wet and discolored.

6 To display the Double Chocolate-Dipped Strawberry and Herb Tree, place it onto a decorative platter or even a cake stand. Surround it with more chocolate-dipped berries and some rosemary or bay leaves or colored ribbons and candles. The tree can be made in the morning and stored, lightly covered in plastic wrap, in the refrigerator until ready to display and serve it. Be sure to tell your guests to remove and discard the toothpicks before consuming.

HANDY HINTS

If you are serving a large number of people, make a forest of strawberry trees in different shapes and sizes to display on your table or buffet.

Double Chocolate-Dipped Strawberry and Herb Tree

DECORATIVE SQUASH SERVING BOWLS OR FLORAL CENTERPIECE

Acorn squash makes a perfect and ideal container for culinary delights such as soup. You can even stuff squash with a cheesy Alfredo bean and vegetable stuffing. As a non-culinary alternative, use squash as a naturally appealing floral centerpiece!

BEFORE YOU BEGIN

The natural combination of fresh flowers and greenery arranged inside an acorn squash picked fresh from the garden, adds warmth, beauty and creative style to any room that it graces. The simple sculpting of the squash turns it into a unique bowl that is sure to delight family and friends. Use the same instructions to create a decorative bowl, add fresh flowers, and it quickly becomes a floral centerpiece beautiful enough to grace the dining room table. Instead of using the squash for a centerpiece it can become a decorative serving bowl for many culinary treats. This great craft is truly multifunctional!

TOOL NEEDED
❑ LARGE CHEF'S KNIFE

MATERIALS NEEDED
❑ ACORN SQUASH
❑ FLORIST'S FOAM
❑ FRESH FLOWERS
❑ LEMON LEAVES OR
   GREENERY
❑ INGREDIENTS FOR
   RECIPES

HOW TO MAKE DECORATIVE SQUASH SERVING BOWLS OR FLORAL CENTERPIECE

1 Find an acorn squash that has a very stable base or create one by slicing off a small portion of the bottom to ensure that it will stand without tipping over.

2 Cut off the top one third of the squash. Remove all seeds and strings from the inside. Carve a ¾-inch-deep zigzag or scalloped pattern around the top edge of the squash.

TAKE NOTE

The outer shell of the acorn squash is very hard; be sure to take extra care and time when slicing it. It is a good idea to have a large, sharp chef's knife.

The centerpiece would also look good with dried flowers preserved from the garden.

3 Cut the extra flesh of the squash away from the opening. At this point the squash is ready to be used as a decorative serving bowl. Use the recipes given or create your own.

4 To make the squash into a floral centerpiece, pack it with florist's foam. Creatively position larger flowers into the foam and then repeat with smaller flowers. Start from the outer edge of the squash and work your way to the center. Add greenery in between the flowers as desired. Embellish with candles or ribbons and bows, if desired.

RECIPES

Acorn Squash Soup

3 tablespoons olive oil
1 cup chopped onion
$\frac{1}{2}$ cup chopped carrot
$\frac{1}{2}$ cup chopped celery
2 pounds acorn squash, cooked, peeled and mashed
1 cup chicken stock
$\frac{1}{4}$ teaspoon nutmeg
$\frac{1}{4}$ teaspoon ground white pepper
1 cup heavy whipping cream
$\frac{1}{4}$ cup chopped Italian parsley

Heat the oil in a Dutch oven over medium-high heat; add onion, carrot and celery and cook until vegetables are tender, stirring frequently, about 5 minutes. Add the cooked squash, chicken stock, heavy cream, nutmeg and pepper. Reduce heat to medium and cook until hot and thickened, about 20 to 30 minutes. Serve soup in acorn squash bowls and garnish with chopped parsley.

TAKE NOTE

Always be sure to set the floral centerpiece on a decorative serving platter for display to avoid any moisture from the squash leaking onto a buffet or table.

Stuffed Squash

1 to 2 medium-sized acorn squash
2 tablespoons butter
1 large onion, chopped
2 carrots, cut $\frac{1}{4}$ by $\frac{1}{4}$ by 1 inch
1 large red bell pepper, cut into 1-inch pieces
15-ounce can garbanzo beans, rinsed and drained
$\frac{1}{4}$ teaspoon coarsely ground black pepper
$\frac{1}{8}$ teaspoon salt
$\frac{3}{4}$ cup refrigerated Alfredo sauce
$\frac{3}{4}$ cup fresh bread crumbs
1 tablespoon olive oil

TAKE NOTE

This craft can also be created using small pie pumpkins or even mini pumpkins in place of the acorn squash.

Heat oven to 325°F. Cut the top off the acorn squash and scoop out all the seeds and stringy pith. Slice a small portion from the bottom of the squash to ensure that it will stand without tipping. Melt butter in large saucepan over medium-high heat. Add onion and carrot and cook until tender, 5 to 8 minutes; add bell pepper and beans and season with pepper and salt. Stir in Alfredo sauce. Spoon vegetables into squash bowls. In small bowl, stir together fresh bread crumbs and olive oil. Cover the vegetables with the bread crumb mixture. Replace the lid on the squash and bake until squash is tender, about one hour.

FRAGRANCE

*M*ost craft creations are for the eyes' enjoyment. But garden themes offer an opportunity to cater to a different sense— what you can smell! This chapter shows you how to treat your nose to a variety of sensory delights, from subtle herbal arrangements to bold and unique potpourris, and from a scent-filled flower basket to fragrant homemade soaps and more. The ideas are grand, the instructions clear, and the results will be delightful.

FRESH AND FRAGRANT HERBAL ARRANGEMENTS

Use an arrangement of fresh herbs to send a decorative message.

BEFORE YOU BEGIN

Herbs have a language all their own. Use mixed varieties to create beautiful, fragrant arrangements filled with meaning. It is easy to grow many herbs at home, giving you the freshest-possible material to work with. Here's how to achieve herb-growing success:
• Grow herbs in a sunny south- or east-facing window.
• To prevent herbs from drying out as they grow, mist them frequently with fresh water. There is no need to feed them.
• Harvest herbs frequently to promote new growth.
• Pick herbs in the summer, just before they begin to flower.
• The longer the stem of the herb, the easier it will be to work with.

TOOL NEEDED
❑ SCISSORS

MATERIALS NEEDED
❑ WIRE FRAME
❑ FLORIST'S WIRE
❑ VARIOUS FRESH HERBS

Herbal Meaning

Herbs are used not only for flavor and fragrance, in decorations and for medicinal purposes—they also have a language all their own.

HERB	MEANING	HERB	MEANING
Allspice	Compassion	Lemon Balm	Sympathy
Angelica	Inspiration	Lemon Verbena	Enchantment
Basil	Love, good wishes	Marjoram	Happiness
Bay	Glory	Mint	Warmth of feeling
Chamomile	Humility	Oregano	Substance
Chervil	Sincerity	Parsley	Festivity
Cloves	Dignity	Rosemary	Remembrance
Coriander	Hidden worth	Rue	Grace
Dill	To lull	Sage	Good health
Fennel	Strength, flattery	Sorrel	Affection
Lavender	Devotion	Thyme	Courage

Herbal Hints
• Sage is very pungent—use it sparingly so that it does not overpower the fragrance of the other herbs in the arrangement.
• Avoid using rue, as many people are allergic to this herb.
• As the fresh herb arrangement dries out, pick off the herbs and use them in recipes.
• Fresh herbs make a wonderful addition to a wedding bouquet.

HOW TO MAKE THE WREATH

1 Lay out all herbs on work surface and cut all stems to same length. Divide into several equal-sized bunches. If you wish, use florist's wire or twist ties to tie bunches together to make arranging easier.

2 Position wreath frame hollow side up. Hold a bunch of bay leaves against frame; wrap florist's wire around bunch and wreath five times to secure bunch. Leave 2 inches of wire free at end; do not cut wire.

3 Working clockwise from top, keeping bunches overlapping in same diagonal direction, continue wiring herb bunches to frame. The wire will be hidden with each successive bunch of herbs. Do not cut wire.

HANDY HINTS

Many flowers have meaning too. Choose some appropriate dried blooms and use them to add color and interest to the herbal arrangement.

4 Continue wiring bunches to completely cover frame. Last bunch should be full enough to cover first bunch. Cut wire, leaving an extra 2 inches at the end. Wind ends of wire together to secure. Make a wire loop and attach to back of wreath for hanging.

Bright Ideas

Use herbs to make fragrant swag and bundles. Select the herbs based on color, texture and their symbolism for a very special gift.

Glorious Swag

• Bay leaves, the symbol of glory, are interspersed with a variety of herbs for an informal swag.
• Mix rosemary, oregano, bay and thyme for a varied combination of light and dark greens. Adorn with dried red peppers and poppy seed heads for color.
• Roll sphagnum moss into a long cylinder. Bunch herbs into same-sized groups and wire onto base; work from each end toward center.
• Knot a piece of raffia around middle to cover the overlapping stems.

Bundle of Love

• Combine beautiful colors and textures to create a wonderful hanging decoration.
• Combine lavender, mint, rosemary, bay leaves, thyme, lemon verbena, artemisia, poppy seed heads and dried red peppers. Arrange herbs in bunches.
• When positioning herbs, keep in mind the bundle will be viewed from below.
• Wrap wire around longest stems below flower heads. Add a second, denser bunch with flower heads slightly lower. Continue adding bunches.
• Add a ribbon bow to cover wire and complement arrangement.

MAKING FRAGRANT POTPOURRI

Perfume your whole house with the wonderful scent of potpourri.

BEFORE YOU BEGIN

Potpourri can be sweet or spicy, depending on the ingredients. Use the recipes below or mix and match your own ingredients from the lists that follow, for a totally unique fragrance and display.

Fragrant flowers include: lavender, Provence roses, damask roses, wallflower, chamomile, verbena, hyacinth, narcissus, sweet violet, lilac, sweet pea, freesia and jasmine. Colorful flowers include: unopened rosebuds, hydrangea, goldenrod, larkspur, peony, marigold, pansy, nasturtium, heather and buttercup. Fragrant herbs and spices include: lemon verbena, rosemary, thyme, sweet basil, sweet marjoram, bay, mint, cinnamon, nutmeg and cloves. Perfumed oils include: rose, lavender, rose geranium, sandalwood, lemon verbena, cedarwood and eucalyptus.

Perfumed Oils

Perfumed (or essential) oils usually provide the dominant fragrance in a potpourri. Essential oils are available at many drugstores and natural body care stores. The oils are highly concentrated, so only a few drops are required. Store the oils in dark bottles, away from heat and sunlight. Keep oils out of the reach of children, and do not allow them to come into contact with skin.

TOOL NEEDED
- ❏ MORTAR AND PESTLE

MATERIALS NEEDED
- ❏ MIXED DRIED PETALS, BUDS, LAVENDER AND LEAVES
- ❏ MIXED FRAGRANT DRIED SPICES
- ❏ DRIED ORRIS ROOT POWDER
- ❏ PERFUMED OIL
- ❏ AIRTIGHT JAR
- ❏ LARGE BOWL

A Potpourri for All Seasons

NAME	INGREDIENTS
Spring Citrus	Lemon-scented geranium leaves, lemon verbena leaves, mimosa flowers, myrtle leaves, grated peel of two lemons, orris root powder, citronella oil, rose oil, geranium oil.
Summer Rose	Dried rose petals, dried marjoram, dried lavender, pepper berries, crushed dried orange peel, orris root powder, rose oil, lavender oil.
Spicy Autumn	Dried apple slices, rose hips, star anise, cloves, juniper berries, sweet gum balls and bark, pine needles, red peppers, cinnamon sticks, oak moss, assorted seed balls and pods, allspice oil.
Woody Winter	Cedar twigs, cedar bark shavings, sandalwood shavings, orris root powder, cedarwood oil, sandalwood oil.

HOW TO MAKE FRAGRANT POTPOURRI

1 In a large bowl, mix together all the petals and leaves, except for the pepper berries and lavender. Combine ingredients from one of the recipes, or mix and match to suit your taste.

2 Use a mortar and pestle to crush the pepper berries and lavender. Crushing releases their scent. Add all the spices and mix well. Pour the crushed materials into the bowl and mix well to combine.

3 Sprinkle 2 teaspoons of dried orris root powder over the ingredients and mix well. Orris root acts as a fixative and helps the potpourri hold its scent. Add two drops of fragrant oil to the potpourri; mix well.

4 Place the potpourri in an airtight jar and store for four weeks. Shake the mixture gently every few days. After four weeks, open the jar and check the scent; add a couple more drops of fragrant oil if desired. Display the potpourri in a pretty china bowl.

HANDY HINTS

If the fragrance of your potpourri begins to fade, place it in the bathroom or kitchen for a few days. Moist atmospheres release the natural fragrance of many plants.

TAKE NOTE

Do not be tempted to use toilet water instead of essential oils to perfume your potpourri. The alcohol it contains will cause the fragrance to evaporate quickly.

Bright Ideas

Mix colors and perfumes for a seasonal potpourri, or combine similar-scented materials for a delicious, room-filling aroma.

Winter Warmth

Set the stage for the holidays with a pine-scented bowl of potpourri by the front door.
• Pinecones, canella berries, honesty, seed pods and fir leaves offer wonderful color but not much scent. Add some dried spices and a few drops of pine oil for seasonal fragrance.
• Wood shavings look pretty and are great for absorbing perfumed oil. Look for red-dyed shavings to enhance the color theme.
• Pull the pinecones and seed pods to the top of the dish to add visual interest.

Fragrant Pomander

Scented pomanders are beautiful to look at and add delicate fragrance to freshly laundered towels in the bathroom.
• Dried lemon peel has a wonderful scent. Combine it with lemon balm leaves and a few drops of lemon verbena oil for a delightful citrus-scented potpourri.
• Glass pomanders have small holes in the top to allow the scent to permeate the room. Moisture in the bathroom will help keep the fragrance fresh.
• Hanging the pomander enables the scent to diffuse more freely.

SPECTACULAR SUNFLOWER BASKET

Use one of the humblest products in your garden—a sunflower seed head—to create an unusual basket for dried potpourri or other decorative natural materials.

BEFORE YOU BEGIN

This basket is perfect for gift giving either empty or with the fixin's inside. A group of three will form an attractive centerpiece on any table or buffet. Because the seed heads are grown rather than manufactured each will be a slightly different shape or size, creating more interest.

It is so simple to make, it's a ten-minute project once the materials are assembled. No practice or weaving required. Just stand back and accept compliments.

MATERIALS NEEDED

- ❏ LARGE SUNFLOWER HEAD
- ❏ PIECE OF WOODY VINE, FOURTEEN TO EIGHTEEN INCHES LONG
- ❏ DRIED MATERIALS TO DECORATE THE BASKET, LIKE LEMON LEAF (SALAL), ORANGE OR LEMON SLICES, ROSE HIPS, SMALL CONES, COCKSCOMB, PINK PEPPER BERRIES
- ❏ DRIED MATERIALS TO FILL THE BASKET, LIKE WHOLE POMEGRANATES AND WHOLE ORANGES

TOOLS NEEDED

- ❏ HOT GLUE GUN AND GLUE STICKS
- ❏ FLORAL SHEARS

HOW TO MAKE A SUNFLOWER BASKET

1 The seed head must be perfectly dry before starting. All the other materials should be dry as well.

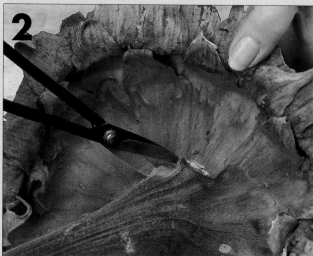

2 Cut the stem of the sunflower off as completely as possible; this makes a nice hollow, which forms the basket.

3 Gently bend the vine, cut to the appropriate size, and glue to the interior of the sunflower head. Most vines twist around each other as they grow. This strengthens the handle and provides an interesting texture. If picked during growing season the vine will be pliable and bend easily. If picked in the winter, allow it to soak in hot water for eight hours and it will be perfect for use.

4 Start gluing materials on the rim of the basket near one end of the handle; a few leaves first and then the larger items like lemon slices. End with smaller items like cones, pepper berries, cockscomb and rose hips. You can decorate the entire rim, two sides of the handle base, or just one side as here. This decision will partly depend on how much decorative material you have and also on whether you plan to fill the basket or leave it empty. Add a leaf or two and a few choice items to the handle, slightly down from the top on one side for additional color.

5 Add dried fruits like whole pomegranates and oranges. Tuck in a leaf or two among the fruit. The contents of the basket can be changed at will. It's pretty on a powder room shelf with extra small soaps or small toiletries, for example.

Sunflower Power

Sunflower Power

There are tons of varieties of sunflowers available from seed catalogs, each with its own set of assets. The dwarf varieties like 'Teddy Bear' are perfect for children or for a mixed border. Choose 'Italian White', 'Velvet Queen', 'Autumn Beauty' or 'Sunny' for a cutting garden. 'Sunbright' with its medium-sized heads and short bright gold petals is the best flower for a dried bouquet and is gorgeous as a cut flower. But for baskets, as well as for humans and birdseed, there's nothing like the heirloom 'Russian Mammoth'.

The stalks are Jack-in-the-beanstalk high at 9 to 12 feet and the heads are huge. 'Miriam Edible' also has very large seed heads. Even if you're growing to eat you might be able to spare one or two to make a basket. Pick as soon as the petals shrivel and the seeds form, so they will adhere tightly even when fully dried. Pick a few days later and the seeds want to drop and will scatter all over your table as you make the project. An alternative is to let the seeds mature completely, brush them out for the birds and use the seedless pod for the basket. If the basket loses a few seeds here and there, however, the look is all the more interesting.

Drying Orange and Lemon Slices

You can purchase whole and sliced dried citrus in craft stores and in floral supply departments. But if you want to make your own dried slices select small fruit with thick skins, the opposite of what you would need for eating or juicing. Slice evenly about $3/8$ inch thick. Blot on both sides with a paper towel to remove excess juice.
• **Spread parchment paper** or wax paper on a baking sheet (to aid in clean up).
• **Place the slices in a single layer** on the sheet and put in an oven at the lowest temperature. This will be about 140 to 160°F. The object is to dehydrate, not bake, the fruit. Check in about two hours. If the fruit seems dry on one side turn it over and continue to dry with the reverse side up for about another two hours. You may want to put down clean paper before drying on the second side.
In any case don't put the slice over a syrupy spot on the paper.
• **Total drying time will be about five hours**, but there are lots of variables including how many slices you dry at one time, how juicy the fruit was, how thick the slices. If you see the first signs of browning remove the fruits from the oven and let them continue to air-dry naturally in a warm spot for a few days.

HANDY HINTS

Use greens like pine, boxwood or arbivitae as a base for the basket. They will nestle in right among the branches.

TAKE NOTE

If you choose to use shellac spray, which helps seal the seeds and keeps them firm, do so in a well-ventilated area after cutting off the sunflower stem.

SCENTED PAPER CASTING

Paper casting is an easy and efficient way to create a fabulous handmade craft. In this technique, the addition of scented oils will produce one-of-a-kind papers that are as fragrant as they are fun.

BEFORE YOU BEGIN

It will not take long to learn how to master the art of paper casting. The techniques are easy enough that even the kids will want to learn how. A small amount of scented oil is added to the paper pulp mixture making these creations smell as good as they look. They make excellent additions to a gift box or become beautiful and unique cards for gift giving.

1 To make paper pulp using linter paper, wet one sheet of paper and tear into pieces; place the pieces into a blender. Add 1 quart cold water and 1 teaspoon paper clay and blend. Pour the pulp into a strainer to drain and let sit until the water stops running and begins to just drip. The mixture will be very wet at this point. Stir in four to six drops of the scented oil. To make paper using recycled papers, cut, tear or shred the paper using a paper shredder; soak the paper in just enough water to cover. Add 1 teaspoon paper clay to the mixture and process the soaked paper in the blender. Stir in four to six drops of scented oil. Pour the pulp into a strainer to drain and let sit until the water stops running and begins to just drip.

TAKE NOTE

Cotton linter paper is a cotton paper that comes in sheet form and can be purchased from a papermaking supplier or craft store. It is made of short fibers that create a soft paper and works well for casting as well as making sheets of paper.

Paper clay is a product that stabilizes the linter paper and can be purchased at craft stores in the papermaking section.

Scented oils can be purchased at most supermarkets or co-ops.

2 Press the pulp into the mold, completely covering the edges, then gently press the pulp into the mold with the sponge. Wring out the sponge and repeat. Using a kitchen towel, press the pulp firmly in the mold to absorb more water and to impress the mold pattern into the paper. Dry the pulp completely in the mold. The length of time it takes will depend on the amount of water left. Sometimes it will take overnight to dry.

3 When paper is completely dry, carefully lift the edges using a thin, sharp knife and pull it away from the mold. Paint or decorate as desired with paints or markers.

EUCALYPTUS WREATH

Create a fragrant eucalyptus wreath and accent it with flowers.

BEFORE YOU BEGIN

With its varying shades of green and blue, fresh or preserved eucalyptus creates a wonderful backdrop for virtually any flower. Consider color, size, texture and longevity when choosing accent materials.

A focal point is created with a colorful ribbon bow tied at the top or a cluster of colorful flowers covering one side of the wreath.

Choose flower colors that will stand out well against the eucalyptus branches. Whether your wreath is fresh or dried, natural or blue, flowers in the yellow, peach and pink families stand out dramatically.

Let a fresh wreath dry naturally as it hangs. Use flowers that dry well, grouping them in small bunches around the wreath.

A grouped design is created when various flowers are tied in bundles to be attached to the wreath. Lay them in the same clockwise or counterclockwise direction as the branches.

An even placement is created when individual flowers are dotted throughout the wreath. Mix flower colors and sizes evenly for interest and balance.

Accent Tips

- Dried flowers are available in colors from soft to vivid and will last for several months.
- Fresh flowers add fragrance and a soft, delicate texture.
- Small collectibles create wreaths with a theme. Consider baby rattles, toy cars or holiday ornaments.
- Choose floral, ribbon and trimming colors to coordinate with the room's color scheme.

TOOLS NEEDED

❑ CRAFT SCISSORS
❑ HOT GLUE GUN AND GLUE STICKS

MATERIALS NEEDED

❑ 18-INCH WIRE WREATH HOLDER
❑ THIN-GAUGE GREEN WIRE
❑ FLORIST'S PICKS
❑ FRESH EUCALYPTUS
❑ FRESH LAVENDER
❑ FRESH BABY'S BREATH
❑ SIX FRESH ROSES

HOW TO MAKE A EUCALYPTUS WREATH

1 Measuring from top of branches, cut several stems 6 to 8 inches long. Group together five or six stems. Include smaller leaved top stems and larger leaved center stems in each group. Keep ends at top of bunch uneven in length.

2 Wrap wire around base of bunch to secure; do not cut wire. Position bunch on wire wreath and wrap wire several times around both, securing stems to wreath; then cut wire. Continue securing, overlapping until wreath is covered.

3 Measuring from top of lavender, cut several stems 6 to 8 inches long. Group three or four stems in a bunch and glue together at base. Wire onto wreath using Step 2 directions. Also glue small bunches of baby's breath randomly to wreath.

5 Spacing evenly, inset the floral pick into the wreath, nesting the rose securely between the eucalyptus bunches. Position the rose stems so the flower faces outward or upward—not straight down.

4 Cut stems of roses to 2 or 3 inches in length. Remove any leaves or thorns. Securely wrap floral pick wire to stem of each rose. Wooden picks provide a sturdier base than natural stems when securing flowers into eucalyptus wreath base.

Bright Ideas

Use the same basic wreath design to add a delicate fragrance or touch of romance to any room you choose.

Fragrant and Colorful

For an everlasting wreath, combine eucalyptus dipped in glycerin and bunches of dried baby's breath.

• The moisture of a steamy shower will diffuse the minty scent of eucalyptus throughout the room.

• Eucalyptus colors differ, due to the process used for drying or preserving. The bluish tone here is attributed to the glycerin.

• For splashes of bright color, tie strands of raffia paper to the stems of the eucalyptus branches. Look for colored raffia in craft stores.

Delicate and Feminine

Create a romantic accent by adding a variety of dried flowers and a sheer ribbon bow to a 21-inch wreath.

• Choose an assortment of dried flowers including pink statice, rat's tail statice, rose-buds, sea lavender, baby's breath and strawflowers.

• Look to the flower colors in the wallpaper or colors in the bed linens and room accessories when choosing dried flower colors.

• A multicolored organza bow adds the finishing touch. Let some ribbon tails hang straight and curl the others.

NATURAL HOMEMADE SOAP

This old-fashioned soap-making technique helps you create glycerin-rich soap in unlimited sizes, shapes and scents, and can be decorated to give as a special gift for special occasions.

BEFORE YOU BEGIN

The natural soap-making process of mixing oil or fat with alkali to create soap is called saponification. The most commonly available oils used in soap making are olive oil, coconut oil and white palm oil, and the alkali is lye or sodium hydroxide. Using simple kitchen and outdoor utensils, your own selection of natural oils, garden herbs, essential oils and household lye, you can create a unique soap that your friends and family will love. Each kind of oil has its own unique property in the finished soap. You can combine different quantities and types of oil to make soap for your special needs. For example, coconut oil creates great lather but tends to dry the skin. Olive oil also creates great lather and is a great skin moisturizer but tends to make soft soap. Palm oil or tallow create nice hard soap that doesn't get soggy in the shower but doesn't lather very well. Each of the herbs you add to the soap has similar properties. By varying the amount of oil, scent and herbs in the soap, you can make soap for dry skin, oily skin and so on.

Because you will be using lye, there are a few important safety tips that must be followed. Always wear gloves and safety glasses to protect your skin and eyes from splashes. When preparing the lye solution, work in a well-vented area. The range vent above the stove works very well. Always work on a vinyl tablecloth or protective surface to prevent damage to your countertops and sinks. Be careful not to spill raw soap on unprotected surfaces, as it will etch the surface. To prevent your pipes from clogging never put raw soap down your sink drain. With this in mind you are now ready to measure, melt and cool your ingredients, mix them together to create soap, pour the raw soap into molds, process, dry and decorate your soap.

TOOLS NEEDED

- ❏ ELECTRIC STICK BLENDER OR WOODEN SPOON
- ❏ KITCHEN SCALE THAT CAN WEIGH UP TO 4 TO 6 POUNDS IN OUNCES
- ❏ A LARGE PLASTIC OR GLASS MIXING BOWL WITH POUR LIP
- ❏ SMALL PLASTIC BOWL FOR MEASURING THE LYE
- ❏ TWO PLASTIC MIXING SPOONS OR SPATULAS
- ❏ TWO CANDY THERMOMETERS (MAKE SURE THEY DETECT AT LEAST DOWN TO 100°F)
- ❏ PLASTIC SOAP MOLDS OR OTHER SPECIALTY SOAP MOLDS
- ❏ LARGE PICNIC COOLER
- ❏ EMPTY MILK OR POP CONTAINER FILLED WITH HOT WATER
- ❏ RUBBER GLOVES
- ❏ SAFETY GLASSES
- ❏ GLASS MEASURING CUP
- ❏ VINYL PICNIC TABLECLOTH OR OTHER SURFACE PROTECTOR
- ❏ WIRE DRYING RACK

MATERIALS NEEDED

	12 BARS	12 BARS (NO TALLOW)
COCONUT OIL	8 OUNCES	8 OUNCES
PALM OIL	8 OUNCES	12 OUNCES
TALLOW	4 OUNCES*	NONE**
OLIVE OIL	24 OUNCES	24 OUNCES
DISTILLED WATER	16.5 OUNCES	16.5 OUNCES
RED DEVIL LEWIS LYE	5.8 OUNCES	5.8 OUNCES
ESSENTIAL OIL (OPTIONAL)	1 TABLESPOON	1 TABLESPOON
DRIED OR CRUSHED HERB TO COMPLEMENT SCENT (OPTIONAL)	1 TABLESPOON	1 TABLESPOON

*TALLOW MAKES A NICE HARD SOAP. IT IS OBTAINED FROM MELTING BEEF SUET, FOUND AT MOST MEAT MARKETS

**MAKES A NICE HARD SOAP WITHOUT USING ANIMAL PRODUCTS

HOW TO MAKE NATURAL HOMEMADE SOAP

1 Measure, melt and cool the ingredients. Using a kitchen scale and a large plastic bowl set scale to zero and measure the required quantities of oil into the bowl. Some oils will be liquid and can be poured into the bowl. Other oils will be solid at room temperature and you will need to use a scoop, stiff spatula or ice pick (if frozen) to get them out of their containers and measure them into the bowl. Measure accurately, within the half-ounce. Place all oils in the same bowl and microwave for 2 to 3 minutes, stirring occasionally until all solid pieces are melted. Place a thermometer in the melted oil. Don't allow the oil to heat above 140°F. Cool the oil at room temperature (or add ice cubes to a cool water bath in the kitchen sink) until it is at 105°F.

While the oil is being melted and cooled, measure the distilled water into a glass measuring cup. Place cup on a protective surface and set under the vent fan above your stove. Turn the vent fan on to remove any fumes that may be generated when the lye is added to the water.

Wearing rubber gloves and safety glasses, measure the lye. Keep the gloves and glasses on for the remainder of the soap-making process. Pour the measured amount of lye slowly into the water while slowly mixing with a plastic spoon or spatula. Stir the lye slowly until all the lye dissolves into solution. Put a thermometer in the lye solution. The solution will heat up to about 180°F when the water and lye are mixed. Place glass measuring cup with the lye solution in the cool water bath and allow temperature to cool to 105°F. Try to cool both the lye and the oil so that they reach 105°F at the same time.

2 Mix the ingredients together to create soap. When both the oil and the lye solution are at 105°F, remove the containers from the cool water bath and set on protected surface of countertop. While stirring the oil slowly with a plastic spatula or spoon, slowly pour the lye solution into the melted oil. The oil will turn cloudy and creamy in color. Continue stirring until all the lye solution is added.

Then using the electric blender stick to stir the soap, blend until the soap mixture forms a "trace" on the top of the raw soap. Many soap recipes will trace in about 5 minutes when using the blender. Tracing is noted by dripping the soap mixture from the spoon in a short line on the surface of the raw soap. When it forms a visible line or "trace" on the surface of the raw soap mixture, the soap has reached its "tracing" point. Another indication that soap is ready to trace is when it reaches the "runny pancake batter" consistency. Essential oil and crushed, dried herbs can be added as an option at this point. Because there is still unprocessed lye in the raw soap the herbs will turn a light brown or rust color. Stir the soap mixture just enough to ensure that the essential oil and herbs are well mixed.

3 Pour the raw soap into molds. Use a larger mold that divides the soap into multiple square bars or individual molds that are used for single bars of soap. Make sure the molds are clean and dry before you use them. When the soap reaches the trace point, pour the raw soap into the mold. Pour it about 1 to 1½ inches thick. Make sure the lid doesn't touch the soap. Cover the mold with the lid and place it in the prepared cooler for 24 hours.

HANDY HINTS

Purchase molds at craft stores or use old food containers. Follow the manufacturer's instructions for pouring and releasing when using purchased molds. When selecting a mold, the only important criterion is that the mold must be plastic with a lid and should create a bar of soap about the right size to fit in your hand.

TAKE NOTE

Never add the water to the lye; it will bubble over and may damage the countertop. Always add lye to the water only.

4 Process the soap. About 30 minutes before the soap is to be processed, prepare the cooler by placing a milk bottle or soda bottle filled with hot water in it and close the lid. The raw soap must be maintained at a warm temperature to ensure the reaction between the oil and lye solution completes. Keeping the filled soap molds level place them in the warm cooler. Be sure the container is level to ensure equal thickness on all sides of the bar. Close the lid of the cooler and keep it closed for twenty-four hours.

After processing for twenty-four hours, remove the single soap molds and place them in the freezer for about two hours. This helps solidify the soap so that the bars will pop out of the mold. After two hours in the freezer, remove the molds, hold them upside down and press the bottom and/or pull sides of the mold until the soap falls out of the mold. For the large, multiple-bar molds, simply slip the divider pieces out of the mold. You may have to use pliers to pull the divider out of the soap. If the soap sticks to the divider or the mold, slide it off. Don't pull it off or the soap may break or become misshapen. Cut soap into desired bar size. Each bar will need to dry for at least twenty-four hours to ensure that the lye solution is completely expended. Put the soap on a wire rack to air-dry.

TAKE NOTE

Wipe the raw soap off the utensils and bowls with a paper towel and throw the towel away. Rinse the lye solution off the dishes with copious amounts of water. Wash all the utensils and molds in the dishwasher after wiping off all the raw soap.

5 Dry the soap. Air-dry the soap for at least 2 to 4 weeks before using it. The longer the drying period, the more solid the bar will remain after it gets wet again. Use soap recipes that use the lye solution to exhaustion to ensure that the soap will not be harsh. This also ensures that there will be small quantities of unprocessed oil left behind and this will act as a moisturizing agent.

HANDY HINTS

Make or buy a small basket and put a decorated bar of soap and a shower puff together as a small gift. Never wrap the soap in plastic as the soap needs to breathe and stay dry to maintain its quality.

TAKE NOTE

For those with sensitive skin, leave out the scent and herbs. If you want to test your skin to see if it will react, wet your fore-arm and rub a bar of soap on the wetted area to leave a soap film on your skin. Leave the soap film on your arm for an hour or two (if it doesn't get itchy) and then wash it off. If your skin does not react you are good to go and can enjoy many hours of show-ering luxury!

6 Decorate the soap. Use fancy or plain paper and crimp it to give it flair. Add ribbon, braid or buttons. Use stamps to embel-lish the label and color the stamp with colored chalk, pencil, or markers. Find a stamp of children in a bubbly tub or some other bathtub theme. It's fun to layer the papers and use trimming scissors to sculpt the edges of the paper. You can create labels on the com-puter too. You can make authentic soap labels, or use humorous names, like *Grandma's Shower Soap, Wedding Shower Soap,* or *Garden Party Soap* for the soaps you make to give as party favors for a birthday, a wedding shower or a garden party. Include pic-tures or stamps appropriate for the occasion on each soap label. If you have a picture of your favorite flower or garden spot, it will be great fun to put the picture on the soap label. People love to get a gift with their picture on it and often save it to display for long peri-ods after receiving it.

The Advantages of Homemade Soap

You will really appreciate the glycerin-rich soap that results from this process. Most commercial soap makers remove the glycerin that is formed in the natural soap-making process to use in other products. People who use their own homemade soap often comment on softer skin and fewer problems with dry skin. Soap is also a great gift idea. You can make it ahead of time and it will keep for many months as long as it is stored in an area that is dry and cool. Soap will easily store for a year or more. Add scent or herbs to the soap that you plan to give as a gift. Essential oils or other fragrance oils made specifically for soap can be found at most craft stores. Grow and dry rosemary, lavender, spearmint, peppermint, and lemon balm to add to your soap too. The scented soaps add a great smell to the bathroom or other areas where they are displayed. The additives can be personalized for each person's taste.

GIVING

*L*ife is filled with occasions big and small
that present opportunities for gift-giving.
And a gift made with your own hands,
attention, thought and time is always the
most meaningful. So when you need to
create something special for someone special,
turn to this chapter. From lovely bookmarks
to an attractive garden gift box and more,
these ideas and instructions will lead you to
two kinds of gift-giving success — a perfect
craft you'll make with ease, and a perfect
gift the recipient will treasure.

A book is like a garden
carried in one's pocket.
~Chinese Proverb~

PRESSED FLOWER BOOKMARK

If you are a gardener and enjoy reading, this is a perfect project for you, to give as a gift or to make for yourself.

BEFORE YOU BEGIN

Some gardeners grow several varieties of flowers in their gardens that are exclusively for pressing, including pansies, violets, and daisies. Fortunately, now you can purchase pressed flowers at most craft stores as well. This project combines the beauty of pressed flowers with the wide variety of colorful and beautiful printed and handmade papers available at craft and scrapbooking stores. In fact, choosing papers for this project is not unlike being out in the garden picking the perfect bouquet. Start with the pressed flowers, and then choose papers and ribbons in color combinations that are visually exciting to you. You will end up with a small, yet delightful, work of art.

1 With specialty scissors, cut the five layers of the bookmark (excluding the printed quote layer), starting with the largest.

Here are the approximate sizes, starting from the largest to the smallest:
$6\frac{1}{2}$ inch by 3 inch (purple polka dots)
$6\frac{1}{4}$ inch by $2\frac{5}{8}$ inch (plum handmade paper)
$5\frac{7}{8}$ inch by $2\frac{1}{4}$ inch (yellow striped paper)
$4\frac{3}{4}$ inch by 2 inch (black and white polka dots)
$4\frac{1}{4}$ inch by $1\frac{3}{4}$ inch (Victorian printed paper).

The idea is to cut the papers so that the lower layers frame the edges of each succeeding layer, so that all the papers are showing.

2 Starting with the first (or bottom) layer, dab a small amount of rubber cement in the middle of each of the layers and lay them one on top of the other.

3 Using the hole punch, punch a hole through all five layers near the top.

4 Choose a favorite quote or write one of your own. On your computer, choose a size and font that you like. Print a trial copy of the quote, and cut it down to see if it will fit under the 4th layer. When you are happy with the size, print it on the 6th paper. Cut it to approximately 2 inch by $1\frac{3}{4}$ inch, and tuck it under the 4th paper. Dab a small amount of rubber cement in the middle and tap down lightly.

5 Laminate the two pressed flowers with at least $\frac{1}{2}$ inch of laminating paper past the outside edges of the flowers. Press down the laminating paper to seal, being careful to avoid wrinkles in the laminating paper. Cut a little excess off the laminate, leaving approximately $\frac{1}{4}$ inch beyond the outside edges of the flower. Using the hole punch, punch a hole near the tops of the flowers.

6 String two of the ribbons, approximately 16 inches each, through the hole in the bookmark, with the long 'tail' coming out the back, and about 1 inch folded over the top in the front. With a hot glue gun, dab a small amount of glue to the insides of the ribbons, and glue them together.

7 Hot-glue the back of silk leaf to the front of the ribbon, right next to the top of the bookmark. String a laminated pressed flower through the wire end of the silk leaf, and twist the wire closed. Wrap the tail of the silk leaf wire around a large nail or a pencil for a curly effect. Tie a small bow around the ribbon, right above the top of the bookmark, and cut off the excess. Tie one of the laminated flowers at the end of a long ribbon.

HANDY HINTS

Don't laminate the front of any of the papers because the handmade papers have such interesting textures. Depending on the papers you choose, you can laminate the back of the largest, or bottom layer for added strength.

Many scrapbooking stores now have work areas, where you can use their specialty scissors and other supplies, if you buy your paper from them.

MUFFINS, BISCUITS AND SCONES FOR GIFT GIVING

Fresh-baked breads, no matter what flavor they are, offer home-style comfort for any occasion.

BEFORE YOU BEGIN

What better gift to give than a warm, fragrant and delicious home-baked treat? You can do it with these recipes, when you creatively package them and let the recipient do the baking!

1 Quick bread mixes are so easy and satisfying to create. There are many ways to package them so they look as good as they taste. For each recipe simply layer the dry ingredients in clear cellophane bags or clear resealable bags.

2 Include the instruction for each recipe with the dry ingredients. This can be done by making labels for the front of the bags, (photocopy the recipe below) and stapling them to the top of the bag or inserting them into each bag. Embellish the bags by fastening small bows or decorations to the top of each bag.

Candied Ginger and Chocolate Chip Muffins

2 cups all-purpose flour
½ cup sugar
½ cup mini chocolate chips
1½ tablespoons crystallized ginger, finely diced
3 teaspoons baking powder
¾ teaspoon salt
¾ cup milk
⅓ cup oil
1 egg

Heat oven to 400°F. Spray a 12-cup muffin pan with nonstick cooking spray. Combine flour, sugar, chocolate chips, crystallized ginger, baking powder and salt in large mixing bowl. Combine milk, oil and egg in a separate small bowl. Add to the flour mixture and stir until mixture is moistened. Divide batter equally in the prepared muffin pan. Bake until toothpick inserted in center comes out clean, about 20 to 25 minutes. Cool two to three minutes and remove from pans.

Cheesy Chive Biscuits

2 cups all-purpose flour
¼ cup grated Parmesan cheese
¼ cup dried chives
2 tablespoons sugar
1 tablespoon baking powder
½ teaspoon salt
¼ cup shortening
⅔ cup heavy cream
⅔ cup sour cream

Heat oven to 450°F. Spray a baking sheet with nonstick cooking spray. Combine flour, Parmesan cheese, chives, sugar, baking powder and salt in large mixing bowl. Using a pastry blender, cut in shortening until mixture is crumbly. Stir together heavy cream and sour cream in small bowl until mixed. Add to flour mixture and combine until moistened. Drop dough by tablespoonfuls onto prepared baking sheet. Bake until golden brown, about 10 to 12 minutes.

Cinnamon Oatmeal Scones

1½ cups all-purpose flour
¾ cup rolled oats
¼ cup firmly packed dark brown sugar
2 teaspoons baking powder
¼ teaspoon salt
¾ teaspoon cinnamon
¼ teaspoon nutmeg
½ cup butter, cut into small pieces
½ cup half and half

Heat oven to 375°F. Lightly grease a baking sheet. Combine flour, rolled oats, brown sugar, baking powder, salt, cinnamon and nutmeg in large bowl and mix well. Using a pastry blender, add the butter until mixture is crumbly. Add the half-and-half and stir until moistened. Gently knead the dough on a lightly floured surface. Place onto prepared baking sheet and press into a six-inch round circle. Cut into eight wedges and separate slightly. Bake until golden brown, about 25 to 30 minutes.

A Garden View for You

GARDEN GIFT BOX

Give a garden gift to a friend who loves being in the garden all year round. You don't need to be outside to appreciate the beauty of the outdoors and a lovely garden!

BEFORE YOU BEGIN

This three-dimensional gift box holds the best images of any special garden. Starting with photographs you may take in the garden, you can line, silhouette, multiple print and collage images to create a lasting memory of a special friend's garden, or one of your own. Move images as you wish, and change them anytime to keep in season, or even to add ideas of what you want your dream garden to be.

TOOL NEEDED
❏ SCISSORS

MATERIALS NEEDED
❏ A BOX, WOODEN OR CARDBOARD CIGAR TYPE
❏ PHOTOGRAPHS (BEST PRINTED ON DOUBLE WEIGHT PAPER)
❏ FLORAL ADHESIVE TAPE
❏ GLUE STICK
❏ RIBBON OR CUT STRIPS OF PAPER
❏ MINIATURE VASE WITH REAL FLOWER BLOOM

HOW TO MAKE A GARDEN GIFT BOX

1 Begin by choosing a box that will hold the photos you plan to use. Choosing photographs, think of those that will give a three-dimensional look. Some images can be multi-printed to cut and paste in creating this dimensional sense. Photos can be cut to size to fit the inside surface of the box. Some images can also be collaged to fit together, to cover all surface area.

2 Starting from the back of the box, insert photos, using floral tape to adhere in place. Using adhesive floral tape gives you the advantage of moving and changing photos as you work. Continue to line the box, top, bottom and, finally, sides.

3 Once all photos are in place, step back and look inside, getting an idea of what can be added as a silhouette form to make a shadow box effect. Cut out any photos you may have that can be added to the front of the box to create this three-dimensional effect. Leave a 1-inch tab on the bottom of any front silhouette image to fold and insert under bottom photo. If the silhouette image does not stand up in place, a small strip of cardboard can be added onto the back for extra support.

4 Ribbon or strips of paper in width of the box edge can be measured to cover outside dimension. Cut edges at 45-degree angles to finish off corners. Use glue stick to glue in place. Extra ribbon can be added to make a bow or decorate outside of the box.

HANDY HINTS

Leave the outside of the box as a plain surface or decorate it with photos or wrap in gift wrap for added appeal.

5 As a finishing touch, add a miniature vase and favorite cut flower. Cut herbs or flowers can also be dried and placed inside as a sachet.

Garden Gift Box

163

PRESSED FLOWER VOTIVE CANDLES

Pressed flowers seem to capture the magic of warm summer days all year long. This is an easy decoupage project, yet the effect is simply beautiful.

BEFORE YOU BEGIN

While you can purchase pressed flowers at many craft stores, you may want to experiment pressing flowers from your own garden. Flowers can be pressed in the back of a book, in a flower press, or even in the microwave.

1 Cut the white mulberry paper so that it will fit around the votive candle. If you are using a more rounded surface, like a hurricane lamp, you can rip or cut the mulberry paper into smaller pieces to fit around the curves.

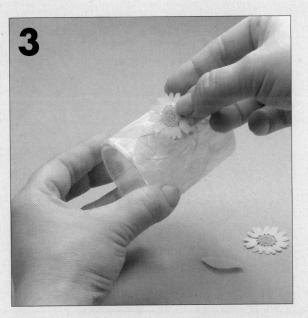

2 **3**

2 Apply a moderate amount of Mod Podge to the outer surface of the votive candle. Place the white mulberry paper around the candle holder, and press down. Wrinkles are okay, but flatten them out using your finger, and then the paintbrush. If you are using smaller pieces of paper, keep adding them, covering the entire surface. Overlapping is okay also. If necessary, trim any excess paper from the top and bottom of the votive candle. Let this dry about 10 minutes.

3 Depending on the size of your pressed flowers, cut out three small leaves from the lime green mulberry paper for every pressed flower. Apply a moderate amount of Mod Podge to a smaller area, lay down a pressed flower, and tuck three leaves around the flower. Using the paintbrush, lightly tap down the flower and leaves with the Mod Podge until they are flat. Continue this process until you have covered the entire candle holder. Let this dry about 15 minutes.

TAKE NOTE

Never leave candles unattended.

4 To seal, apply another coat of Mod Podge, which will dry clear and give a glossy finish to the surface.

5 Add a tea light candle.

BASKET OF GARDEN FLOWERS

You can make your own basket or you can buy a basket to fill with your favorite summer garden flowers. Dry your favorite garden flowers so you can enjoy them in the fall and winter too.

BEFORE YOU BEGIN

This project is really two crafts in one. Use your favorite dried flowers to fill a classic market basket that you can make in a day. Baskets are a perfect complement to dried flowers.

There are some general instructions to follow when making any basket. Reed comes in one-pound bundles. Remove the amount of reed needed and retie the bundle for future use. Always soak the reed you will use in cool water for about 5 minutes to make it pliable to work with. While weaving, it may be necessary to rewet the reeds by spraying the reeds with water to prevent them from drying or cracking and to keep them pliable for weaving.

Each reed has a right and a wrong side. When wet, the wrong side has a "hairy" look to it that can be noticed when the reed is bent over your finger. Always weave the wrong or hairy side of the reed on the inside of the basket so that the smooth side faces out and enhances the look of the basket.

Reed can be dyed to add interest and color. Use powdered or liquid dye. Follow the directions for dye preparation, except add double the water and a cup of vinegar or salt to set the dye. Use a large, old pot that you don't care about staining. Reed should be separated from the original bundles before dyeing, rerolled, and tied into small, loose, wreath-like bundles. Add small bundles of reed to hot dye and soak for about 10 to 20 minutes depending on darkness of dye preferred. After soaking the reed in dye, rinse the reed in cold water (laundry sink works best) until dye no longer appears in rinse water. If you splash the dye while working with it, clean it up with a weak solution of bleach water. One package of dye is enough to dye about 2 pounds of reed. Rewet dyed reeds when ready to use. Wipe with a paper towel before weaving to avoid dye bleeding into the undyed reeds.

TOOLS NEEDED

FOR DRYING FLOWERS:
- ❏ DRYING RACK
- ❏ WOODEN DOWELS
- ❏ RUBBER BANDS
- ❏ GARDEN CLIPPER

FOR THE BASKET:
- ❏ REED CUTTER
- ❏ SCREWDRIVER
- ❏ CLOTHESPINS
- ❏ TAPE MEASURE
- ❏ OLD TOWEL
- ❏ PENCIL
- ❏ UTILITY KNIFE
- ❏ WATER SPRAY BOTTLE
- ❏ SMALL PAINTBRUSH OR SPONGE BRUSH
- ❏ LARGE BOOK TO USE AS SPOKE WEIGHT
- ❏ TABLE OR COUNTER TOP TO WEAVE ON

MATERIALS NEEDED

FOR DRYING FLOWERS:
- ❏ YOUR FAVORITE FLOWERS OR HERBS SUCH AS LARKSPUR, LAVENDER, GLOBE AMARANTH, GLOBE THISTLE, GERMAN STATICE, STATICE, BABY'S BREATH, SAGE, OREGANO, PRAIRIE GRASS WITH INTERESTING HEADS OR FOLIAGE AND HYDRANGEA

FOR THE BASKET:
- ❏ ³⁄₄-INCH FLAT RATTAN REED FOR SPOKES
- ❏ ¹⁄₂-INCH FLAT RATTAN REED FOR WEAVERS AND FILLERS
- ❏ ¹⁄₄-INCH FLAT/OVAL RATTAN REED FOR WEAVERS
- ❏ ⁵⁄₈-INCH FLAT/OVAL RATTAN REED FOR RIM
- ❏ SEA GRASS
- ❏ 10- BY 14-INCH PRE-MADE OAK HANDLE
- ❏ MINWAX STAIN AND TURPENTINE OR MINERAL SPIRITS

HOW TO MAKE A BASKET OF GARDEN FLOWERS

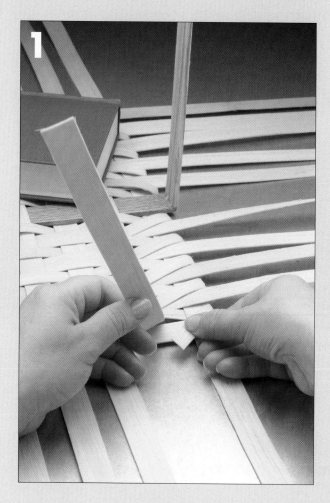

1 Cutting the reed and forming the base of the basket:
Using the reed cutter, cut the ¾-inch reed into seven spokes each 34 inches long, and ten spokes each 29 inches long. From the ½-inch flat reed, cut ten filler pieces 16 inches long. After soaking the spokes, find the wrong side of all the spokes and mark in the middle of each spoke on the wrong side. Horizontally in front of you on the table, lay four of the 34-inch spokes wrong side up, matching the middle marks and placing the spokes about 2½ inches apart. Place the 10- by 14-inch pre-made handle over the four spokes, matching the middle of the handle with the middle marks on each of the spokes and the edge of handle base with the outside edge of the outside spokes. Lay the three remaining 34-inch spokes horizontally on the top of the handle and between the first four spokes, again matching the middle marks. Place a large book (or spoke weight) on one side of the handle over the spokes to hold the spokes in place.

Using an over-under weave, weave one filler piece in the opposite over-under pattern as the handle, matching the middle marks and pushing the filler right next to the handle. Weave one 29-inch spoke in the opposite over-under pattern as the first filler matching the middle marks and pushing the spoke right next to the filler. Continue weaving the four fillers and four spokes in the same pattern, matching the middles and weaving the fillers and spokes right next to each other. Bend the filler pieces at an angle away from the handle so that they can be tucked under the adjacent spoke. Trim the filler at a slight angle before tucking if necessary.

Remove the book from the other side of the basket and repeat the pattern with the remaining five fillers and spokes on the other side. You should now have a flat base with an upright handle. The handle should be treated as a spoke. Each spoke should have about ½ inch of open space between them on the sides of the basket and about ½ to one inch between them on the ends of the basket. Measure the base to ensure that it is about 10 by 14 inches with 7 inches of base from the end of the basket to the middle of the handle. Adjust the base so all sides are even to ensure that the basket will be balanced on each side after weaving. Spray spokes with a water spray bottle if they appear to be drying out.

2 Upsetting the spokes and forming the sides of the basket: Using a pencil, number each side of the basket using numbers 1-4. Upset all spokes by softly bending at the edge of each side. Push down lightly with your thumb. You may hear a slight crackling sound, but don't worry, that's part of the mystique of basket weaving.

Using the over-under, start-stop weave, and using clothespins to hold the weaver in place, weave four rows of $\frac{1}{2}$-inch flat reed. Spokes should be kept at a 90-degree angle to the base of the basket. Start on side 1 and move to the next side with each new row. This ensures that the basket will have an even shape. By the fourth row you will no longer need to use the clothespins to hold the weavers in place. Be sure to soak the weaver before weaving so that it is pliable. Remember to weave the wrong side of the reed toward the inside of the basket.

Weave eleven rows of $\frac{1}{4}$-inch flat/oval reed using the over-under, start-stop weaving. The flat side of the reed is the wrong side on the flat/oval reeds. (Optional: Instead of eleven rows of plain $\frac{1}{4}$-inch reed, you can use two rows of colored reed, seven rows of plain or a second color, and two rows of the first-color reed to add a little color to the basket. You can experiment with the color pattern.) Weave four more rows of $\frac{1}{2}$-inch flat reed using the over-under, start-stop weave. The fourth row will become a false weaver. Be sure to pinch all the rows tightly together as you weave and before going to the next step.

3 Finishing the top edge of the basket: With the reed cutter, trim off the inside spokes just below the top edge of the false weaver. Cut the tip of the outside spokes at the angle of a picket fence so that the spoke fits under the second weaver from the top. Spray the spokes if they are dry. Bend the outside spokes downward at the top edge of the false weaver. Bend the spoke over your finger to produce a curl in the spoke. Tuck the spoke under the second weaver. The tucking of the spokes over the false weaver will now hold all the previous rows of weaving in place. Bend an extra long $\frac{1}{4}$-inch flat/oval reed over about two inches from the end with the wrong side up. Place the bent end, wrong side up, over the edge of the basket, between two spokes and between the handle and the front of the basket. Hold it in place with a clothespin. This will become the lashing piece.

Using the utility knife, scrape off the oval side of the $\frac{5}{8}$-inch flat/oval reed on one end for about three inches to create a flat area on the end of the reed. Use this end of the reed to start the inside of the rim. Place the wrong side of the $\frac{5}{8}$-inch flat/oval reed on the inside front of the basket over the false weaver. Hold it in place with clothespins. Start the end on top of a folded-over spoke rather than a cut-off spoke. Pin the reed in place all around the inside of the basket and over the false weaver and overlap the area scraped with the utility knife. Cut the rim at an angle. Slip sea grass under the clothespins and adjust it so that it is sitting on top of the false weaver and against the wrong side of the inside rim. Cut the sea grass so that it butts up to the handle on either side. Scrape the $\frac{5}{8}$-inch flat/oval outside rim piece as you did the inside rim piece. Start the rim on the opposite side of the basket, on the outside of the false weaver holding it in place with a clothespin. Continue pinning the rim all around on the outside of the basket and overlap the area scraped with the utility knife. Cut the rim at an angle. You should now have the inside rim, outside rim and sea grass in place over the false weaver of the basket and over the tip of the lashing piece.

HOW TO MAKE A BASKET OF GARDEN FLOWERS

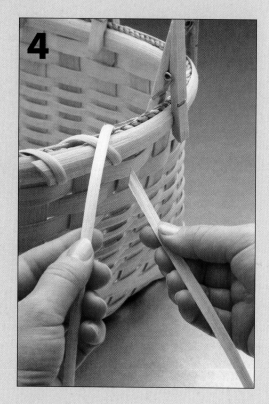

4 Lashing the rim to the basket: In the previous step, the end of the lashing piece was anchored under the rim of the basket. Trim the other end of the lashing piece to a point. Make sure the lasher stays damp by spraying it occasionally with water. Using a flathead screwdriver, poke a slight hole in between each spoke and in between the last weaver and the false weaver. Force the pointed end of the lasher into the area opened with the screwdriver and pull it through completely until it tightly holds the rim in place. Be sure to keep the reed straight so that the wrong side of the flat/oval reed is always flat against the rim. Continue lashing all around, pulling the lasher tightly so that the rims are held firmly in place. When you come to the handle, lash backward one spoke to form an X over the handle on each side and then lash over the first part of the X a second time. When you come to the cut angle of the overlapping inside or outside rim, trim the angle so it matches the angle of the lasher and the lasher barely covers the cut end. Continue lashing all around the basket until you come to the starting point. Using the point of the lasher, poke it up under the bottom side of the rim, between the basket and inside rim. Pull the lasher until it is very snug. Poke the lasher under the sea grass (you may have to lift the sea grass slightly with the screwdriver) and under the top side of the outside rim, between the basket and the outside rim. Pull the lasher snug again and readjust the sea grass. Trim off the start and the stopping point of the lasher at the bottom of the outside rim and tuck it under the outside rim with the tip of the screwdriver. You are now officially finished weaving the basket. Turn it over and add your initials and date with a pencil to document this one-of-a-kind basket. You may also want to number each of your unique creations. Remember each basket is as unique as the basket weaver is. It is really hard to create an exact duplicate. Shape the bottom of the basket with your hands while it is still damp to ensure that it sits on its four corners and to ensure that it doesn't rock or wobble. You may have to push up or create a "hump" in the middle so that the basket rests on its corners. Let the basket dry for at least a week before staining.

TAKE NOTE

If you have a perennial and annual flower garden you can collect seeds and cut flowers throughout the summer. Then you can make baskets in the winter. Make small jam jar baskets and berry picking baskets for party favors and fill with flowers, jam or just a colorful dinner napkin. Attach a "memory tag" to each basket with a stamp or picture appropriate for the occasion. Baskets are great gifts for family and friends. The addition of dried flowers from *your* garden to *your* handmade baskets makes them very special for the recipient.

5 Staining the basket: Use Minwax to stain the basket. There are also other craft wood stains that will work. The golden oak stain color is buttery, light and very popular, but there are a large variety of colors depending on your own personal tastes. A natural color looks like the basket was not stained. Mix equal parts of stain and mineral spirits or turpentine. Then brush the stain mixture on the inside of the basket with a small paintbrush or sponge brush. Cover the entire basket on the inside and out. Be sure to do the bottom and the handle as well. After staining, set the basket on a nonporous surface to dry. Try not to use too much stain or it may drip down the basket, causing the bottom of the basket to be darker than the top. The stains smell for a week or so, so try to keep it in a well-vented area or in the shop.

TAKE NOTE

If you really decide that you like basket weaving, there are tools that are made specifically for basket weaving. The correct tools make the process a little smoother for those that plan to do this more often. The three tools most recommended are a reed cutter, a lashing tool (instead of the screwdriver) and the basket scraper (instead of the utility knife). The supplies for basket weaving are available from several places on the Internet. Also, there are lots of great patterns in many craft books.

TAKE NOTE

Although dried flowers aren't collectibles, they are great for decorating. Use them in vases, wreaths, wall sconces, floral buckets and so on. The list is endless.

Drying the Flowers and Filling the Basket

The garage is great for drying flowers. It's cool, dry and usually free from wind. Nail several ½-inch by 4-inch by 30-inch boards to the wall. Then drill ¼-inch or ⅜-inch holes about 6 to 8 inches apart to hold wooden dowels. Stick the dowels in the holes. Then as the flowers are ready to dry, cut bunches of them, wrap the ends with rubber bands and then hang the bunch of flowers on the dowels by the rubber bands. After about 2 to 3 weeks the flowers are dry and ready to arrange in a basket. Mix and match the variety and color of the flowers and arrange them in the basket. In time the flowers start to fade, so refresh them with a new supply from the garden each year.

INDEX